DATE DUE

DEMCO 38-297

SHAQUILLE O'NEAL

SHAQUILLE O'NEAL

Ken Rappoport

walker and company ✳ new york

First published in the United States of America in 1994 by Walker Publishing Company, Inc.

Published simultaneously in Canada by Thomas Allen & Son Canada, Limited, Markham, Ontario

Library of Congress Cataloging-in-Publication Data
Rappoport, Ken.
Shaquille O'Neal / Ken Rappoport.
p.   cm.
Includes bibliographical references.
ISBN 0-8027-8294-9 —ISBN 0-8027-8295-7 (lib bdg)
1. O'Neal, Shaquille.   2. Basketball players—United States Biography.   I. Title.
GV884.O54R37   1994
796.323'092—dc20
[B]   93-38561
CIP

Book design by Ron Monteleone

Printed in the United States of America

4   6   8   10   9   7   5   3

To all my beautiful children: Felicia and David, Sharon and Richard, and Larry

CONTENTS

ACKNOWLEDGMENTS

The author is grateful to the following for their help with this book: Ford McMurtry, Marcus George, Dale Brown, Dave Madura, Joel Smith, Kent Lowe, Brad Messina, Lee Feinswog, Herb More, Joe Cortez, Charlie Bennett, Sam King, Barry Cooper, Louis Torres, Joe Cavallero, Scooter Hobbs, Ed Murphy, John Hunt, Joe Dean, Sue Harper, Ben Abrams, Doug Sandberg, Darren Mathey, Sue Rowland, Ray Stubblebine, Rusty Segler, Danny Henderson, Robby Dunn, Jim Hawthorne, Brian Cazeneuve, Richard Olson, Jimmy Martin, Henry Baker, John Hines, Dave Flores, Marcia Davis, Bill Kruger, and Pat Williams.

Thanks again to Mary Perrotta Rich, my editor at Walker and Company, and to my favorite home editor, my wife, Bernice.

SHAQUILLE O'NEAL

1 SHAQ ATTACK

"Shaquille O'Neal attacked the basket like no one I've ever seen. I want to see the guy who would even think of attempting to block one of his dunks. I guarantee he would break his hand if he tried it." —Cleveland Cavaliers forward Mike Sanders

---

The pressure was almost unbearable. Shaquille O'Neal was only a rookie, yet everyone was counting on him.

It was the last weekend of the season, and the Orlando Magic's final chance for a playoff berth. O'Neal, who had signed a $40 million contract, had been the focal point of the season. Now he was the focal point of the weekend.

A sellout crowd filled New Jersey's Meadowlands Arena. The Magic-Nets game was one attraction. The other was O'Neal, the Magic's sensational young center. He had just turned twenty-one. At seven feet one inch tall and 300 pounds, O'Neal's physical presence suggested raw power. His strength was becoming legendary— along his career path lay bent rims, shattered backboards, and broken baskets. But that's not all that made him unique. Just as impressive was his agility for a basketball player that size.

O'Neal's talents had turned around a sorry franchise. In the previous three years of their existence, the Magic finished far out of playoff contention. In O'Neal's first season, they were a contender. But to qualify for a postseason berth, victories in the last two games were essential. Otherwise, the Magic's season was over.

The air was electric as O'Neal and his teammates took the court. The Magic had been hoping to blow open the game with an early rush, but they couldn't manage it. With three minutes left in the first period, they trailed 25–21. They needed a jump start, and they got it from O'Neal.

O'Neal took a pass from Anthony Bowie on the right baseline and flashed past Dwayne Schintzius, the Nets' seven-foot-two center, toward the basket. O'Neal ducked inside and soared into the air over the Nets' Derrick Coleman.

Slam dunk! The explosive force left the Magic center hanging on the rim, momentarily suspended in midair.

The heavy metal brace supports of the basket assembly wobbled, then snapped. The crowd gasped as the 90-pound clock, which sits atop the backboard, swayed. It came smashing down directly over O'Neal on the court below. Frantically, the players scattered to safety. O'Neal ducked and rushed away as the stanchion, the backboard, and the basket toppled and slammed to the floor with a resounding crash.

Everyone looked on in disbelief. O'Neal, who was slightly grazed on his shoulder by the clock, pinched his right arm and signaled he was okay. He walked past the crippled backboard and joined his teammates. They congratulated him as the crowd went wild. The Nets were in a state of shock.

Finally, both teams were ushered off the court to the thunderous applause of 20,049 electrified fans.

This was the second time O'Neal had made NBA history. The first occurred two months earlier against the Phoenix Suns. In the Magic's first nationally televised game, O'Neal astounded everyone at the new America West Arena. Minutes into the game, his forceful slam dunk crippled the custom-made basket support. The basket folded, swayed, and collapsed in a heap.

"All that was missing was Tarzan's yell," one columnist wrote.[1] It was the first time in NBA history a player dunked hard enough to bring down a basket—giving new meaning to the oft-used phrase "Shaq Attack."

While bringing down the basket, O'Neal brought up the TV ratings. Viewers watching the game were mesmerized. O'Neal generated new fans for himself, the Magic, and the publicity-conscious NBA.

When play resumed in New Jersey, O'Neal sank a free throw to cut the Nets' lead to 25–24. He had been fouled on his dunk shot. The rest of the game belonged to teammate Nick Anderson, who scored a franchise-record 50 points. Yet O'Neal still managed to make an impact. His basket-breaking performance broke the momentum of the Nets. Then, with the game tied and 1:07 to play, O'Neal blocked a driving layup by Drazen Petrovic. The Magic won 119–116 to stay alive in the playoff race.

Two days after playing their worst game of the season, a 28-point loss in Boston, the Magic had won one of their biggest. The next game was crucial. Shaquille didn't mind the pressure. His growing-up years had prepared him.

2 ARMY BRAT

''If it wasn't for my father, I think I might be in jail now, not in the NBA. He always taught me to do the right thing, to never forget my roots, to never forget where I came from and to never forget that I've been fortunate.''
—Shaquille O'Neal

Shaquille O'Neal never backed down from a dare, and he wasn't about to this time.

"Bet you won't pull it," the boys taunted.

"Oh, no? Watch me!"

Shaquille pulled the fire alarm, then raced down the hallway as fast as he could. An ear-splitting noise filled the building. Two fire trucks and several police cars, their sirens wailing, screeched to a halt in front of the Military Ocean Terminal, a base for U.S. Army personnel in New Jersey.

"Hey, kid!" someone shouted at O'Neal as he

scrambled away. In minutes, he was rounded up by the military police and taken to the station house. A call to his father was the first order.

O'Neal's father was Sergeant Phillip Harrison, who was stationed on the base. He arrived in a hurry, obviously angry and clutching a Ping-Pong paddle.

"Where is he?" Shaquille's father demanded.

One of the MPs motioned to an adjoining room.

"Before you go in there, Sergeant, remember that corporal punishment is against U.S. Army regulations," the MP warned.

"You had better go ahead and write me up," Sergeant Harrison said.[1]

Harrison yanked Shaquille out of the room and paddled him. It was not an unusual scene in the Harrison household when Shaquille was a boy.

"I was bad," O'Neal said. "My parents had to stay on me all the time. My father stayed after me and finally straightened me out. Being a drill sergeant, he had to discipline his troops. Then he'd come home and discipline me."[2]

Luckily for Harrison, he was big enough to handle Shaquille. A broad-shouldered 240-pounder, Harrison never shied away from disciplining his son. Shaquille usually needed it.

"I got spanked every day," Shaquille said. "I had it coming. At the time, I didn't see it. I didn't think my parents loved me."[3]

O'Neal has described his father as "mean." He was certainly hot-tempered. Their relationship has changed for the better over the years.

"The father-son relationship is great today," O'Neal said. "Back then, it wasn't." O'Neal blamed himself for that.

"I was one of those kids who thought they knew it all. My dad was trying to keep me off the streets, to keep me off drugs, trying to make me into somebody. At first, I didn't like it, but it was all my fault. All I had to do was listen. Luckily, I listened before it was too late."[4]

One day O'Neal decided to pick up a basketball.

"I found a way out for myself," he said.[5]

He had help. When his father wasn't disciplining him, he was working with Shaquille on the court.

"My dad used to throw me all kinds of passes," Shaquille said. "He really taught me how to get a feel for the basketball. From then on, I started getting better and better. I just listened to Dad and what he was teaching me about the basics."

Before Shaquille learned the basics, he was struggling. "I couldn't dribble and I couldn't shoot the ball well."[6]

Shaquille couldn't have had a better teacher than his father. Phillip Harrison had played basketball at St. Augustine's College in North Carolina and Essex County College in New Jersey. Harrison was his son's first basketball coach at Fort Stewart, Georgia, when Shaquille was nine years old.

Shaquille was born in Newark, New Jersey, on March 6, 1972. He was destined to be big. Phillip Harrison was six feet five and Shaquille's mother,

Lucille O'Neal, was six feet two. Shaquille's father bought him a football uniform. But Shaquille's genetic makeup was more balanced in favor of basketball.

Phillip Harrison had joined the army in the 1970s. He was shipped out before he could marry Shaquille's mother. So when Shaquille was born, his mother gave him her family name. How he got his first and middle names is an interesting story. O'Neal's birth came five years after the racial riots in Newark, which had caused a national uproar, claiming twenty-six lives and resulting in more than $15 million in damages. The riots started with the arrest of a black cabdriver and then lasted for six days.

During this dark period in Newark's history, the Muslims held many of the neighborhoods together with an emphasis on pride and self-reliance. The Muslims were admired by many blacks in Newark, who expressed their admiration by giving their children Islamic names. Lucille O'Neal named her son Shaquille Rashaun. In Arabic, Shaquille means "little one" and Rashaun means "warrior."

When Harrison came back, he and Shaquille's mother were married. Eventually, they had three more children—LaTeefah, Ayesha, and Jamal.

In Newark, O'Neal's family lived in a low-rent housing project. Many times, they didn't have enough money to buy food. They had to use food stamps to get groceries. Life changed for the better once O'Neal's father decided the family should move away.

O'Neal had mixed feelings about leaving Newark. His grandmother lived there, and he had always considered it home. But, in retrospect, he realized that leaving was the best thing to happen to him.

"There were a lot of temptations in Newark—drugs, gangs. When we lived in the projects, guys would ride by in their Benzes. Kids wanted to have fancy clothes and the Benzes" . . . and would do illegal things to get them. O'Neal didn't want to be tempted to do the same. "The best part for me was just getting out of the city."[7]

As the son of a soldier, O'Neal became well traveled. By the time he was fifteen years old, he had lived in three different regions of the United States—Northeast, South, and Southwest—as well as in Europe. The Harrisons were continually on the move. The family lived, in succession, in Newark, Jersey City, Bayonne, and Eatontown, New Jersey; then briefly at Fort Stewart, Georgia; followed by a longer stay in Germany. Finally, they moved to Fort Sam Houston in Texas. It was a hectic life. No sooner did O'Neal get comfortable in a new school on another army base than he was pulled out and forced to adjust to new surroundings.

"The worst part was meeting people, getting tight with them, and then having to leave," O'Neal said.[8]

Since O'Neal was bigger than most kids his age,

this made him the subject of taunts and jokes. "I always got teased about my size," he said. "I used to be ashamed because I was tall. And kids would make fun of my name, too. They'd say my name rhymes stupidly and they'd laugh."

His taunting schoolmates called O'Neal "Sasquatch," after the legendary monster. They all got a big laugh out of that at O'Neal's expense.

Finding clothes for their growing son was no laughing matter for Shaquille's parents. "We'd buy him pants on Saturday and by the next Friday, they wouldn't fit," complained his father.[9]

At Fort Stewart, O'Neal got his first taste of organized football. O'Neal was a nine-year-old lineman in a league that featured players up to eleven years old. "He was the biggest player in the league," said Jimmy Martin, sports director of the youth activities program at Fort Stewart. "Teams wanted to check his birth records to see if he was eligible."[10]

At this time, O'Neal appeared to be a better football player than a basketball player. In a punt, pass, and kick competition at the age of nine, he won all three phases.

Basketball had not yet become O'Neal's forte. "He played basketball and kickball, but I had seen a lot of kids with more ability," remembered Henry Baker, who had O'Neal in his physical education class at Fort Stewart Elementary School. O'Neal was "easy to coach, but wasn't that coordinated. He was large and his skill hadn't caught up to his size."[11]

As the son of a soldier, discipline had been a way of life for O'Neal. One day, Baker paddled him for an infraction.

O'Neal's father heard about the paddling and came to school to confront his son's teacher. Harrison was a big, gruff man. He walked up to Baker while he was teaching a class outside. Baker didn't know what to expect.

"Are you Mr. Baker?" Harrison asked.

"Yes, I am."

"I'm Shaquille's father. I understand you paddled my son yesterday."

Hesitating slightly, Baker answered, "Yes, I did."

"Well, I just wanted to come out and shake your hand, Mr. Baker!"

The surprised look on Baker's face led Harrison to explain that the family had just arrived in Fort Stewart. Prior to this, nobody would discipline Shaquille. "I appreciate your disciplining him," Harrison said, and walked out.[12]

Marcia Davis had no such problem with O'Neal in her fifth-grade homeroom class. He was a very manageable, B-average student. Davis found O'Neal to be "somewhat softhearted. Whenever he got in trouble, he always admitted he was wrong."

That was the last Marcia Davis would hear of O'Neal until he was a basketball star in college. The Harrisons soon were on the move again—this time to Germany, where Shaquille would begin to develop his basketball talents.

3 FLOWERING IN FULDA

"He had a lot of confidence in his abilities. He really thought he was a good basketball player. But he never lorded it over anybody."
—Fulda High School athletic director Marcus George, remembering Shaquille O'Neal as a sophomore

Shaquille O'Neal pressed his agonized body forward, his thin legs straining, tears welling in his eyes. The end was in sight.

Another hundred yards, he thought. I must do it. He wore a look of fierce determination as he pushed himself harder into the homestretch. He accelerated, and crossed the finish line with a sudden burst of energy. Then he collapsed on the sideline, gasping for breath.

The scene was almost as painful for Ford Mc-Murtry to watch as it was for O'Neal to run.

"His legs were growing so fast and his muscles were not growing as fast as his bones were growing," McMurtry remembered. "He ran painfully."[1]

McMurtry coached the basketball team at Fulda High School, a facility for the children of military personnel in Fulda, Germany. McMurtry first met O'Neal in the fall of 1986 when O'Neal came out for the basketball team. McMurtry remembered a tall, gawky, determined sophomore trying to persuade a skeptical coach.

"Coach," O'Neal boldly proclaimed, "I'm going to be your center this year."

McMurtry was hesitant. He had seen too many awkward tall boys thinking they could dominate on a basketball court.

"Shaquille," McMurtry said in half-mocking, half-serious tones, "you know you aren't all that great."

"No, Coach, really, I am."

A determined look appeared on Shaquille's face as he pressed his case.

"Shaquille, maybe you think you're the only tall guy to come down the pike. All tall guys think they can play. But they just take up space out there."

"Coach, give me a chance."

The kid deserved a tryout, McMurtry thought, and O'Neal soon proved him right. When the season started, O'Neal was made the starting center for Fulda. Few fourteen-year-olds had more confidence.

Before O'Neal's first game, McMurtry asked, "Shaquille, are you nervous?"

"Coach, I won't ever be nervous," O'Neal replied.[2]

And he wasn't. O'Neal scored 16 points in that game, against players who were two to three years older. O'Neal also had double-figure rebounds. Not bad for a first game.

As a ninth grader, O'Neal had not tried out for the Fulda High School team. He played for a community program in Wildflecken, where he lived.

Marcus George, the Fulda athletic director and guidance counselor at the time, remembered O'Neal at freshman registration when Shaquille walked into his office: "He was about to hit the top of the door. He looked like a giraffe, real long legs and real skinny."

"Are you a football player?" George asked O'Neal.

"I play a little," O'Neal said, "but I think my main sport is basketball."

"I can see why," George said, taking in the large-size youth dwarfing his desk.[3]

O'Neal's size was accompanied by his warm personality.

"He always had a smile," McMurtry said. "He was very engaging and never said a bad word about anyone. He was a gentle giant."

It was an awkward time for O'Neal, who was still learning about himself and about basketball. He showed some potential but had not yet fully matured as a player. While he was tall, his legs were thin and weak. He had only recently taught himself how to dunk. "I had bad knees and couldn't jump over a pencil,"[4] Shaquille remembered.

But O'Neal was determined to succeed. He worked with weights to improve the condition of his knees and his body as a whole. Fear of injury in football had pushed O'Neal toward basketball. "One day one of the football players tackled me in the knee. That told me I should give up football."[5]

Shaquille had other dreams, too: He wanted to be a break dancer. He would imitate his favorite dancers on the TV show "Fame." He once alarmed fellow students in Germany while going through a break-dancing routine. Falling on his back, he started jerking and spinning on the floor. Friends watching the performance thought he was having an epileptic seizure. They ran and called the school nurse. O'Neal's father later heard about the incident when he went to a parents' meeting. Shaquille had skipped class to do the dance routine. His father was so angry he took his son out of the conference room and into the bathroom "and beat his behind."[6] But by his sophomore year in high school, O'Neal had become too big to be a break dancer. He was, however, just right for basketball. He had a wide body six feet eight inches tall with a long wing span, and he was a player who was eager to learn.

"He played hard in practice," McMurtry remembered. "He was always on time. When you taught him something, you could just see him soaking it up. He hung on every word. He was very analytical."[7]

O'Neal's persistence was another personality trait. On road trips, it was mandatory for Fulda players to wear a tie and jacket, complete with dress shoes. O'Neal had unusually large feet. In Germany, he had problems finding shoes large enough, so he painfully squeezed into smaller sizes. As a result, Shaquille looked forward to getting on the bus.

"When he got on the bus, he couldn't wait to take his shoes off," McMurtry said. "He'd go to the back, peel off his shoes, and just relax."

When the bus reached its destination, O'Neal dutifully squeezed his feet into the uncomfortably tight shoes, put on his jacket, and went out with the team as a unit.

"I never heard him complain about the dress code," McMurtry said. "He never asked for any special favors. He never asked for anything above and beyond what anybody else asked."[8]

McMurtry's relationship with O'Neal perhaps went deeper than those of most coaches and players. McMurtry wasn't much older than his players and related to them. He was barely out of Auburn University, where he had been a punter on the football team. He had done some high school coaching in the States.

Originally, McMurtry came to Fulda to coach football at the urging of Marcus George, who was an old friend from the States. But he stayed to coach basketball when the basketball coach quit. That gave McMurtry the unique opportunity to watch O'Neal blossom from an ugly duckling into a swan.

McMurtry had never seen an athlete quite like O'Neal. And it wasn't just his startling size. McMurtry was also impressed by O'Neal's court awareness.

A team from Berlin was playing at Fulda one weekend. It was then that O'Neal made "one of the most incredible plays" McMurtry had ever seen:

He blocked a shot by one of the Berlin players about five feet from the basket. He tipped the ball toward the sidelines where the Berlin team was sitting, then tipped it upcourt again. The ball was directly in front of the Berlin bench. O'Neal dribbled it and looked at the Berlin coach, who was standing on the sidelines in total disbelief that anyone that big could handle the ball that well.

"Watch this, Coach!" O'Neal said to the Berlin coach.

At that point, O'Neal threw the ball behind his back the length of the court with his left hand and hit a teammate in stride. The Fulda player took a step and laid the ball in. Two points!

"Shaquille just turned to me and smiled as he went by," McMurtry said.[9]

And McMurtry smiled back.

4 A SOLDIER'S SON

''Shaquille's crying. He's upset that he has to leave his teammates before the championship finals. I give him a hug and Coach McMurtry gives him a hug, and all the kids give him high fives as he goes out the door.'' —Athletic director Marcus George remembering Shaquille O'Neal's farewell scene at Fulda High School in Germany

At one time, the Fulda Gap was a strategic military point in Europe. Before Germany reunited and the Soviet Union fell apart, the Gap was a cause for concern in the free world. The hilly, seventy-mile terrain was the border that linked West Germany to East Germany. Many thought if the Soviets were ever to invade the

West, they would more than likely come through the Gap.

In 1987, it still presented a problem, as far as the Allies were concerned. But the only gap that Shaquille O'Neal was thinking about at the time was one that had been created by his father and the U.S. Army.

O'Neal had balked at going to Germany, but his years there turned out to be a positive experience. He had developed his athletic ability and at last felt a part of something special. As a sophomore, he was the key player in Fulda High School's hopes for a berth in the postseason Small Schools basketball tournament.

For three years, life in the military community in Germany had been pleasant enough for Shaquille. The military children played together in programs run by the army's Dependent Youth Association and were generally insulated from the outside world. During O'Neal's time in Germany, there were few anti-American incidents. Once in a while, local radicals went on a rampage and smeared American tanks and automobiles with bright blue paint. Other than a terrorist activity in faraway Berlin, that was about the extent of the trouble.

Fulda was a relatively new school among those on army bases in Germany. When Marcus George arrived at Fulda as athletic director in 1985, the school was only in its third year and the athletic department was just starting to put its sports teams together. Fulda had to compete with the popular community sports programs for local talent.

O'Neal started playing at Fulda in his sopho-more season, along with others from the commu-nity program in Wildflecken. Fulda soon found its teams filled with fine athletes, both in football and basketball. The school started to do well in both sports, despite being one of the smallest schools in its league. With about 250 students, Fulda would often have to compete with schools nearly twice its size.

In the 1986–87 season, the basketball team re-volved around O'Neal, who averaged about 18 points and 12 rebounds a game. "It wasn't an overall great team," George remembered, "but coach [Ford] McMurtry is a good coach and got a lot out of the kids. They really played their hearts out for him."[1]

As for O'Neal, he handled every obstacle that was put in his path. He was usually at his best in such circumstances. Against one particularly tough rival school, which hadn't lost a game in three years and had beaten Fulda by 27 points ear-lier in the season, McMurtry challenged O'Neal: "Carry us."

He did just that, for at least part of the game. By the half, O'Neal had 16 points, 10 rebounds, and 5 blocked shots. Fulda led by 2. But by the second half, O'Neal's intense play began to take its toll and Fulda lost the game. "The poor kid was just overwhelmed in the second half," McMurtry said. "He gave everything he could and didn't have anything left. But he accepted every challenge. He never complained, never asked why, just went out and did it."

Fulda came on strong at the end of the year and won five of six to qualify for the postseason tournament. "We came in as the favorite," McMurtry said. "Shaquille was a very big part of that."[2]

McMurtry was counting on O'Neal for the playoffs. The U.S. Army, however, had other plans. The army reassigned O'Neal's father back to the States. It was bad timing. O'Neal did not want to leave his team at the most crucial part of the season.

The community was equally devastated, as was McMurtry. McMurtry had many conversations over the next week with Shaquille's parents. He hoped to convince them to let their son fly back to the United States later so he could finish the season. The soldiers in the community mobilized. They so desperately wanted Shaquille to play, they helped raise the $2,000 fare for a later flight home.

McMurtry thought he had everything worked out with O'Neal's parents, until a phone call disrupted his plans.

"You know, Coach, I know how much you mean to Shaquille," Lucille Harrison said tearfully. "I know how much he means to your team. But I just can't leave my baby. He's only fifteen years old, and I can't go across that big ocean and leave him here."[3]

McMurtry understood. The next day, with O'Neal playing his last game, Fulda won. Everyone on the team knew O'Neal was leaving, but no one expected what happened next.

After the game, McMurtry was talking to the team in the locker room when suddenly the door burst open. Phillip Harrison strode into the room.

"I need to take Shaquille," he said brusquely. "We need to go."

"Well, I'm not finished talking to the team," McMurtry told O'Neal's father. "It will be five more minutes."

"Coach," Harrison said, "we need to go *right now.*"

Shaquille, startled to see his father, had turned and walked into the bathroom at the back of the locker room.

"I'll get him for you," McMurtry told Harrison. "Just step outside for a minute."[4]

Harrison left the locker room, and McMurtry walked into the bathroom. He saw O'Neal bending over the sink. McMurtry saw that the sink was wet. O'Neal turned and faced his coach, tears streaming down his face.

McMurtry's heart went out to O'Neal.

"Coach," O'Neal said in a choked voice, "thank you for everything."

Years later, the scene is still vivid in McMurtry's mind.

"I guess at that moment it really hit home that he wasn't going to be with us anymore," McMurtry said. "That was possibly the last time I would ever see him."

O'Neal put his arms around McMurtry and hugged him.

"He held me so tight," McMurtry said. "I could feel his tears dripping on me, down my face."

"Coach, I love you," O'Neal said. "Thank you."[5]

With that, O'Neal left the locker room to meet his father. Phillip Harrison took Shaquille back to the United States and a new start with the Cole High School basketball team in San Antonio, Texas.

5 TALL STORY

''I just looked up one day and here comes this big kid walking into school. My first thought was, 'Boy, our basketball team is going to get a lot better.' ''—Cole High School principal Buddy Compton upon first seeing Shaquille O'Neal

Sue Rowland, a math teacher, walked into her class at Cole High School one day to find a new student. She couldn't have missed him; he was sitting in the front row and his legs stuck out about halfway across the room.

"I do hope you play basketball," she said to Shaquille O'Neal, a twinkle in her eye.

"Yes, ma'am, I do," he replied softly with a grin.[1]

It wasn't until the following year that O'Neal was able to make the team. At the time he arrived, the season was almost over. It was evident at once to basketball coach Dave Madura that O'Neal was special.

"The first week he was at Cole, we went to the gym," Madura said. "We were just kind of messing around to see if he could do anything. I could see right then he was one strong dude. He was going to be a player."[2]

O'Neal's entrance to Cole High School late in his sophomore year was cause for excitement at the military-based school. After meeting with O'Neal and his parents for the first time, Cole athletic director Joel Smith couldn't contain himself.

Madura was sitting in his office when Smith burst in.

"God almighty," he said, "we've got ourselves a giant!"

The giant wore a size seventeen shoe. "Where am I going to get shoes for this kid?" Smith said incredulously. By the time he was a senior, O'Neal shot up to nearly seven feet, and his shoe size along with him. "He went to size twenty. I ordered plenty of them [shoes] in advance."[3]

At first sight, both Madura and Smith were cautiously optimistic about their new player. For years they had seen promising athletes from Europe fall flat. "We got a lot of kids from Germany that were 'all-European' or 'all-Germany,' " Madura said. "The majority of them never panned out because it was a different competition level."[4]

In the mid-eighties, about two or three years before O'Neal had arrived, Cole had struck it rich with an influx of great young football players. The talent had rocketed the Cole Cougars into the state playoffs.

The Cougars' basketball program also had some moments of glory in the eighties. Madura was a big reason for their success. A product of the Texas Panhandle in northern Texas, Madura was a low-key, laconic man with a dry sense of humor and a good sense of basketball.

"He never cracked a smile when he joked. He never moved real quick and he rarely got upset," said Herb More, who played for Madura at Cole and later coached with him. "He was the type to let kids play. He never embarrassed his team on the court. Of course, there were times he let them know how he felt in the dressing room."[5]

While the talent had never been overwhelming at Cole, Madura had managed to put competitive teams on the court since starting at the school in 1979. Just before O'Neal arrived, the Cougars had completed a 21–5 season and reached the postseason playoffs for the third straight year.

Madura had coached few players with O'Neal's size and talent. The closest was Tommy Barker, a six-foot-eleven center who played for Madura at Westlaco, another Texas high school. Barker played college ball at Minnesota and Hawaii, and made it to the National Basketball Association. As Madura remembered, "He was not even close to Shaquille." More, one of the top scorers in Cole history, was another memorable player for Madura, yet he was even shorter than Barker and thinner than O'Neal. Again, not in Shaquille's class.

But who was?

"Shaquille's father brought some videotapes from Germany, and we watched a few," Madura said. "You could tell he was a player. But we didn't want to get too excited. We had been disappointed before."

Before O'Neal started his junior year, Madura put him in a summer league to see what he could do.

"I put him in the third level, which was for decent players, but not the best," Madura said. "I think it took him about two days to decide he didn't need to be playing there."[6]

The fifteen-year-old O'Neal made the summer league all-star team that year.

Louis Torres, who coached O'Neal in summer high school tournaments, remembered his work habits most of all. "The best thing was that he was coachable. He had a great attitude."[7]

O'Neal would very often show up an hour and a half before practice was scheduled to start. Many times, he was the last to leave.

"Coach, what shall I work on?" O'Neal would typically ask.

"In practice, he liked to get into that drip and sweat, really work. The kid wanted to be a good basketball player," recalled another coach, John Hunt.[8]

Hunt found O'Neal to be exceptionally polite and well disciplined. The lessons of life—hard work, discipline, respect for authority—had been drummed into Shaquille by his no-nonsense father. After basketball practice one day, this scene took place between Shaquille and his father:

"Dad, is it okay if I get a hamburger with the guys?"

"What time are you going to be back?"

"What time do you want me back?"

There was no doubt who the authoritative figure in Shaquille's life was. Shaquille stayed late one afternoon to play basketball and didn't let his father know. Not long after, Harrison stormed into the gym at Cole. In a rage, he hauled his son home.

"I don't think I've ever seen his dad quite as angry as he was when he walked into that gym to get Shaquille," said math teacher Rowland. "That's the way their family was run, and I guarantee you, if his father said, 'Be home at five o'clock,' Shaquille was there."[9]

Shaquille's father has been described by family acquaintances as a "military type, someone who's brusque and abrasive." But he has also been described as a caring parent.

When Shaquille needed to make up classwork following his transfer from Fulda, he attended summer school. To Harrison, schoolwork was just as important as basketball, and he made sure his son hit the books as hard as he hit the backboards. It showed in Shaquille's classwork.

"He kept up his lessons in my class and made really good grades," Rowland said. "He enjoyed learning."

When O'Neal was later a renowned basketball

player in college, he dropped by Cole High School to visit with Rowland, whom he called "Mom."

"Mom, I just wanted to let you know I was doing really well in math," O'Neal said as he sat down, putting his arm around Rowland. O'Neal knew that would please Rowland.

"I'm pleased with your basketball," she told O'Neal, "but I'm also pleased with your grades."[10]

O'Neal had received a good foundation for college at Cole, where he was surrounded by an excellent academic environment. The school was perhaps known more for its academic program than for sports—at least, before O'Neal started playing basketball there. On two occasions, Cole had received a National Exemplary School award for all-around excellence from the U.S. Department of Education. It was one of the top high schools in the nation.

Phillip and Lucille Harrison were typical of many of the involved parents at Cole. They regularly attended Cougar Club meetings and, of course, basketball games rooting for their son and his team. During football season, Phillip Harrison could be found dragging yardage chains to measure first downs. It was a family affair. Shaquille's skyscraping figure stood on the sidelines studiously keeping team statistics.

O'Neal was a blend of his parents' strongest qualities. He had his father's fierceness and competitiveness on the court and his mother's gentleness off it. He also had a free spirit of his own and a sense of theater and fun.

"Shaquille wore a Gucci hat pointed up like a shark's fin, a big clock around his neck, and 'Terminator' glasses," remembered Joe Cavallero, a teammate of Shaquille's at Cole. "He'd walk around like that, really noticeable, especially when we went into another town to play a game. He wanted to psyche out the opposition."[11]

On the basketball team, O'Neal was the center of attention, and not only because of his talent on the court. On the bus rides to and from games, he was usually the most vocal and hyperactive.

While Shaquille's weight and height had forced him to abandon his dream to be a break dancer, he could still sing. With high school friends, he made rap videos, Cavallero remembered. "He composed songs."[12]

"Our bus rides were never quiet and reflective," remembered teammate Robert Dunn. "We were always beating rhythms on the seats. Shaq kept us entertained. He was the team clown."[13]

Shaquille was, literally and figuratively, the biggest thing to happen to Cole athletics. Among the 1,200-odd high schools in Texas, Cole was a relatively small school of about 300 with a postage stamp–size gym that seated about 500. When O'Neal played basketball at Cole from 1987 to 1989, a 5,000-seat gymnasium wouldn't have been large enough to accommodate the overflow crowds.

Shaquille was an attraction on the road as well. Wherever Cole played basketball, gyms were packed just to see his specialty—the dunk shot.

Even opponents' fans clapped when he started downcourt, hoping to see one of his rim-bending dunks.

At that time, Rowland was working with the journalism staff at Cole as the basketball photographer. On one occasion, she got so excited watching Shaquille dunk, she forgot to take the picture! O'Neal had that kind of effect on people.

There was a rule in Texas high-school basketball: No dunking in pregame warm-ups. Cole was playing Somerset in the district playoffs when the Somerset athletic director walked into the room where the referees were dressing before the game.

"You'all don't come out until that buzzer goes off," he said.

The referees looked puzzled.

"These people all paid to see Shaquille O'Neal dunking in the warm-ups. No refs now—we don't give a damn about the rules!"[14]

6 THE COLE EXPRESS

"Shaquille was the man in the middle. He took an average bunch of players and brought their level of play up." —Darren Mathey, Shaquille O'Neal's teammate at Cole High School

The bus carrying the Cole High School basketball team rolled along Interstate 35 on the way to Austin for the Texas state championships.

"Look!" someone shouted from a seat in the rear.

"Well, I'll be darned," said another.

All the players pressed toward the window. Hundreds of people stood at a rest area along the road. Shaquille O'Neal's parents were in front holding up a large "Cole Cougar" banner. They all shouted and cheered as the bus went by.

Said Robert Dunn, a Cole player: "That's when it really hit us hard. We were on our way to the state championships. It was a memorable moment."[1]

The season had been quite a ride. With O'Neal the centerpiece, the Cougars were unbeaten in thirty-four games when they reached the state finals in March of 1989. Their victories included a revenge beating of Liberty Hill in the regional championship game. The year before, Liberty Hill had handed Cole its only loss of the season, knocking the Cougars out of the tournament.

Beating Liberty Hill meant a lot to O'Neal. He had blamed himself for the loss the year before. O'Neal missed two foul shots in the closing minutes, which he called "the worst moment of my life."

O'Neal still vividly remembered that bitter loss as the Cougars were getting ready for another Liberty Hill team one year later. The day of the game, Cole coach Dave Madura said he "almost choked" when he read the morning newspapers. O'Neal was quoted as saying, "Liberty Hill cheated us last year."[2]

Oh, my God, how am I going to get around this? Madura thought.

O'Neal never minded saying what he thought. But neither did the Liberty Hill fans. When O'Neal entered the arena for warm-ups, shouts of "We're going to cheat you again, Shaquille!" greeted him.

O'Neal's teammate Darren Mathey described the Liberty Hill fans as "racists." They had called

O'Neal a racially disparaging term. Liberty Hill coach Danny Henderson was not pleased. O'Neal was a tough opponent as it was. Henderson didn't want to see O'Neal any angrier.

"I had a great team that year," Henderson remembered. "It was a frustrating situation. In a normal year, we had a very good chance to get to the state tournament. Shaquille was a big obstacle. We could play him a hundred times and never beat him."[3]

O'Neal had come back as a six-foot-ten, 250-pound senior. Over the summer, he had dominated tournaments sponsored by Basketball Congress International (BCI). An argument with his father sparked one of O'Neal's greatest performances. O'Neal could not remember the subject of the argument. Everyone remembered his performance in the high school all-star game that day. "I just kept dunking and dunking," O'Neal said. "The next day, people were calling me the best center in the nation."[4]

Among those was *Hoop Scoop* recruiting magazine. "He is like a deer just learning to run," said Clark Francis, editor of *Hoop Scoop*. "It is scary how good he could be if he continues to develop."[5]

O'Neal liked the recognition.

"It gives me an extra incentive to improve this season," he said. "They say I'm the best in the country, and now I'll have to prove it."[6]

Madura had put O'Neal on a bodybuilding program, and it was evident he was stronger in his senior year. O'Neal started bending rims with his dunk shots. Because of O'Neal, many of Cole's opponents changed to breakaway rims. It was cheaper in the long run. The schools that didn't switch had problems. In a late-season game against Southside, O'Neal's dunks had bent the rim to such an extent that a teammate left the game shaking his head.

"I can't shoot on that rim; it's like a roller coaster," he complained to Madura.

Liberty Hill coach Henderson had watched game tapes from O'Neal's junior and senior years. "It was absolutely amazing to see the difference. Shaquille went through a physical metamorphosis from his junior to his senior year."[7]

O'Neal was the best player Madura coached in a quarter century in the business. And the Cougars that season were his best team.

"They understood that for us to win, we needed to get the ball to Shaquille," said Herb More, Cole's assistant coach that season.[8]

The Cole team completely changed its style in O'Neal's senior year. When he was a junior, the Cougars had more all-around speed and used the entire court, pressing and running from one end to the other. When he was a senior, the Cougars reduced their approach to a half-court game with O'Neal the focal point.

But although the Cougars featured O'Neal, they were hardly a one-man team. Dwayne Cyrus and Eric Baker, two splendid forwards, were back for another year. More felt Cyrus was the best all-around athlete on the team. "He could run like a deer, throw the football sixty yards, catch the football, knock the baseball out of the park. Some people were afraid to pitch batting practice to him, the way the ball came off his bat."

The stocky Baker, who also played football, had a good sense for basketball and was the perfect complement to O'Neal. He could find him anywhere on the court with his thread-needle passes. Doug Sandburg, a guard, was the best outside shooter on the team, but didn't always look to shoot. By the end of the season, Sandburg had become the Cougars' best ball handler and ran the team with confidence and poise. "He was like an assistant coach on the floor, deciding what tempo to play," More said.[9]

The hard-core nucleus of the Cougars that year also included guards Jeff Petress and Darren Mathey. Guards Joe Cavallero and Sean Jackson also saw a lot of playing time, especially when Petress and Cyrus were lost to the team because of academic problems.

O'Neal was the first to point out the Cougars were not a one-man team. A game against Sweeny proved it. As usual, the Cougars' opponents double- and triple-teamed O'Neal, leaving the rest of the Cole players open for shots. O'Neal only scored 4 points that night but set his teammates up for a lot of easy baskets. Petress led with 25 points, one of the rare nights that O'Neal did not lead the Cougars in scoring. O'Neal blocked some 20 shots as the Cougars won easily, 77–40.

O'Neal's great inside game was complemented

by the Cougars' fine outside shooting. They were ranked first among high schools in their district in 3-point shooting with a 40 percent completion rate. For a 3-point basket, the shot has to be made outside of a designated line, about 20 feet away from the basket; otherwise, it's a 2-point shot. Mathey and Sandburg were among the state's top 3-point shooters.

O'Neal led the team in scoring with a 31.2 points-per-game average, including a 47-point effort against Lampassas that broke More's school record. With O'Neal leading the way, the Cougars were hardly tested in the regular season. They averaged 80 points a game and beat most of their opponents by 30, 40, and sometimes 50 points. The closest the Cougars came to losing happened in Karnes City.

"It was a small rinky-dink arena, like ours," Cole guard Mathey recalled. "There was so much noise, I couldn't hear the ball hit the hardwood. They started scoring from the outside, couldn't miss, and we were down by five at halftime."[10]

The Cougars were in a state of shock, losing 30–25 at the half. It was the biggest lead an opponent had all season. How could this be happening? Their opponents were a smaller school and not expected to win. A highly motivated Cole team came out in the second half. By the end of the third period, the Karnes Cougars had tied the game. Then they outscored the Badgers 15–2 in the fourth period to pull away and hand Karnes its first loss in seventeen games.

"It was a turning point in the season," Mathey remembered.[11] It showed the Cougars had character and could hang tough in tight situations.

This was the Cougars' fourteenth straight road game, all part of Madura's scheme. "I really wanted to get these kids out and around," he said. "It is a good learning experience."[12]

The Cougars had won tournament trophies in Marble Falls, New Braunfels Canyon, and Kerrville. The experience of visiting all those enemy gymnasiums toughened them up for the playoffs, and eventually the state championships in Austin.

7

THE SAMSON COMPLEX

''The thing I remember was the crowd. We looked up in the stands and couldn't believe how many people were there. Then we saw a small section rooting for us.'' —Cole High School player Robert Dunn describing the atmosphere of the state championship basketball game in Austin, Texas, on March 11, 1989

The Cole basketball team was in trouble. With about five minutes left against Clarksville in the state championship game, the Cougars had lost their momentum. Now, it seemed, they were about to lose the lead.

What was worse, they were in danger of losing

Shaquille O'Neal. O'Neal had picked up his fourth foul a few minutes before and was on the bench watching his teammates squander a big lead.

Clarksville had scored 6 straight points and pulled within one, 54–53. At that point, Cole coach Dave Madura was afraid to put O'Neal into the game. It's too early, Madura thought. One more foul and Shaquille is out.

Madura looked at the clock: 5:03 left. In basketball, five minutes can be a long time. But did he have a choice?

"If I put you back in, can you stay away from that fifth foul?" Madura asked O'Neal.

"Yeah, Coach, I can," O'Neal responded.

"Okay, get in there!"[1]

O'Neal had been a big-game player for the Cougars all season. But he was prone to fouls because of his physical style.

"I was hoping to keep him out until three minutes remained," Madura remembered.[2]

Madura hoped O'Neal would respond as he had two days before in the state semifinals. His 38 points, 20 rebounds, and 4 blocked shots led Cole to a 69–56 victory over Hearne. Cole also lost a big lead in that game, allowing Hearne to come within 3 points on three occasions in the final period. But during the last four minutes, O'Neal hit 4 straight jump shots to help the Cougars pull away.

Even at that, O'Neal wasn't particularly happy with his game. He had missed 14 of 33 shots. He was hesitant about going hard to the basket. "The refs were calling charges and it got me scared, kind of nervous," said O'Neal, who confined most of his shooting to about six feet away.[3]

But that was not his style. And he wasn't about to change against Clarksville, foul trouble or not.

He took the court . . .

Before the game, there was a memorable scene in the Cole locker room. Coach Madura broke down, tears streaming down his face. This was a shock to the players. Madura had always been easygoing and calm. He rarely got emotional.

The game was the biggest many of the Cougars would play in their lives. Madura was about to give the biggest pep talk of his life. But something happened on the way to his pregame speech.

"That season was an emotional roller-coaster ride," said Darren Mathey, one of fourteen players on the closely knit Cougar team. "Coach Madura finally let it all out. It was a special moment. He cried. He let us know that next to his family, we were the most important people in his life."[4]

There was no question Madura liked this team. The year before, there had been conflict on a team that was generally considered more talented. But in the 1988–89 season, Madura knew he had a group of players who were willing to go to war for each other. And for him.

He also knew this might be his last chance to win a state championship. He had been coaching at Cole for ten years and chances were he would never coach another player like O'Neal.

Between tears, Madura said:

"Don't win it for yourselves . . . win it for all the teams I have coached."

That short speech "fired" the team.

"I wanted to get that out of the way," Madura said.[5]

Madura usually was not superstitious. But during the 1988–89 season, he refused to get a haircut until the Cougars lost. By the time the team had reached the playoffs, still undefeated, Madura's hair had grown to Samson-length proportions. "I guess it's the Samson complex," he joked,[6] alluding to the biblical story of the strongman whose hair was the source of his power.

It had been more than twenty years since Cole High School's basketball team had reached the state tournament. Cole had made two previous appearances, losing both times. Now the Cougars were just one game away from winning it all. They knew Clarksville was a worthy opponent. Clarksville had won twenty-nine of thirty-one games and beaten Brownfield in the state semifinals.

From the beginning, the state championship game was a tremendous battle. Clarksville's best player, Tyrone Washington, started connecting on long shots. O'Neal went inside and dunked over Washington, pinning him to the backboard.

The teams were close. There were four lead changes and four ties in the second quarter. They left the court at halftime tied at 32.

Madura always carried a towel that he squeezed

or chewed during tense moments in the game. Now was definitely towel-chewing time.

Cole scored 11 straight points in the third period, including two dunk shots by O'Neal, to take a 45–37 lead. Cole led 53–44 at the end of three periods, but Clarksville still had life left. O'Neal suffered his third and fourth fouls in a two-minute span, and Madura pulled his big man out of the game with nearly seven minutes remaining. Back came the Tigers with a rally of their own, generating a huge roar from the record crowd of 13,042 at the Erwin Center in Austin. They outscored the Cougars 7–1 and cut the lead to 54–53 on two free throws by Bennie Jenkins. With 5:03 left on the clock, it was Shaquille time.

O'Neal responded, leading Cole on an 8–0 streak.

He hit an eight-footer. He fed to Dwayne Cyrus for a basket. He intercepted a pass that Sandburg converted for a field goal. Finally, he blocked a shot that led to two free throws by Jeff Petress.

Clarksville was history. Final score: Cole 68, Clarksville 60. The first state championship for Cole!

A happy bunch of Cougars charged into their dressing room. O'Neal was so pumped up, he tackled Dunn on the way in. "I thought he broke my leg!" Dunn exclaimed.

Mathey, meanwhile, was in shock.

"I couldn't move," he remembered. "It took a month to realize that we were it. We were kings.

From every starter down to the water boy, every-body felt a part of it."[7]

For Madura, it was a special moment. Not only was it his first state championship in twenty-five years of coaching, but he could finally get his long-awaited haircut.

8 COLLEGE BOUND

''I just think they trusted us, and the rest was history.'' —Louisiana State University basketball coach Dale Brown after Shaquille O'Neal decided to go to LSU

C ole's state championship was one of two important events in Shaquille O'Neal's senior year. The other event took place before the basketball season.

O'Neal signed a letter of intent to attend Louisiana State University. LSU basketball coach Dale Brown had achieved a significant recruiting victory. Actually, Brown had the inside track. His association with O'Neal and his family went back to Germany. The LSU coach was giving a clinic at an army base when he met O'Neal. That meeting became a part of LSU basketball lore.

Brown was packing to go home. He felt a tap

on his shoulder. Turning, he saw a tall, strapping young man standing before him. It was O'Neal.

"Coach Brown, could I ask you some questions?"

"Certainly," Brown said.

"I don't have good endurance. I don't have a good vertical jump," O'Neal said. "Could you give me some weight program to work on?"

Brown jotted down some exercises for O'Neal, then took his name and address to send him the LSU weight program.

"How long have you been in the service, son?" Brown asked innocently.

"I'm not in the service," he said.

Brown raised an eyebrow.

"You're not? What, are you just visiting?"

"Coach Brown, I'm only thirteen years old."

That was Brown's first introduction to O'Neal, who was about six feet six at the time. The meeting took place in 1985.

"I'd like to meet your father," Brown said.[1]

O'Neal led Brown to a nearby sauna, where Sergeant Phillip Harrison was working up a sweat. Brown was excited. Here was a prospect who would probably be a seven-footer by the time he got to college. He would certainly look good in an LSU uniform.

But Brown didn't get a chance to say much to O'Neal's father. Harrison put his hand up after the LSU coach had barely spoken.

"I'm not all that concerned about basketball," Harrison said gruffly. "I think it's time blacks started developing some intellectualism so they can be presidents of corporations."

Harrison paused.

"If you're interested in my son's intellect, and he develops as a basketball player, we might be able to talk someday."[2]

Brown was given Shaquille's grandmother's address in New Jersey. He corresponded with the family over the next few years. "Little did I dream he would come to LSU," Brown said.[3] When the time came for O'Neal's college decision, LSU was high on the list.

Some of the biggest names in college coaching had visited O'Neal as he prepared for his senior year. Among them: North Carolina's Dean Smith, North Carolina State's Jim Valvano, Louisville's Denny Crum, Jerry Tarkanian of the University of Nevada–Las Vegas, and Lou Henson of Illinois.

Their visits were a tribute to O'Neal, but also a distraction. After O'Neal played particularly well in a summer tournament, Cole coach Dave Madura remembered, "The phone started ringing off the hook. They all came. In fact, we had so many coaches coming, I didn't want to see them anymore. I was getting tired."[4]

O'Neal was tired, too—tired of visiting campuses across the country, tired of the continuous phone calls, and tired of all the mail he kept getting from schools. He estimated he had received about 500 letters.

"Almost every day I had calls from coaches— sometimes telling me about the program, about the gym, about the dorms," O'Neal said. "I told all the coaches, 'Don't call me past ten-thirty.' "[5]

Above all loomed the shadow of Shaquille's father. According to Madura, Harrison "made it clear that he would not tolerate any 'under-the-table' kind of stuff."[6] No amount of money, bribes, or promises could buy his son.

Smith had come in with a long list of players he had sent to the pros from North Carolina, including Michael Jordan. You could be like Mike, Smith told O'Neal. The Harrisons weren't impressed. Nor was Shaquille. "I don't want to be another name on somebody's list," he said.[7]

It was, finally, Brown's straightforward approach that won over Shaquille.

"Coach Brown didn't tell me just what I wanted to hear," O'Neal said. "The other places I had visited were telling me I was the greatest high school player in the country."

Brown, on the other hand, didn't. O'Neal liked that.

"Coach Brown said if I came to LSU and proved myself, I could be a starter. He put the emphasis on my proving myself. The other places were suggesting that I would start if I just showed up. I really did like coach Brown's no-nonsense approach to recruiting. He told me exactly what to expect."[8]

O'Neal had visited North Carolina, North Carolina State, Louisville, Illinois, and LSU. He said the only other school he really considered was Illinois, "but I liked the players and the coaching staff at LSU better."

As a rule, coaches don't enjoy recruiting athletes. It takes time and effort and oftentimes can be discouraging. But Brown found recruiting O'Neal was one of his easiest tasks.

"I knew there wouldn't be many people involved because the father was very strong-willed and would scare them off," Brown said. "There were no games with the family. Just very straightforward. They were very honorable to deal with, which made it pleasant."[9]

O'Neal was named all-city, all-state, and all-America in a variety of publications after his senior year. But playing with a relatively small high school, O'Neal wasn't sure how his talent would match up against players across the country. He found out in April. He played in the Dapper Dan tournament in Pittsburgh, a high school all-star game featuring the best high school players in the country. O'Neal scored 18 points and was named the West's most valuable player.

Then he knew he was as good as anyone on his level.

"I think he'll be a terror in college," said Tim Osteszewski, a senior at Jay High School, one of Cole's rivals. "He's improved a lot since we played each other during the summer of my sophomore year. He's gotten bigger and stronger."[10]

O'Neal couldn't wait to start his college career.

9 PERIOD OF ADJUSTMENT

''I looked at Shaquille as a young, wonderful stallion and yet he had never been in the Kentucky Derby. By the end of the season, he was running pretty well.'' —LSU coach Dale Brown on Shaquille O'Neal's freshman season with the Tigers

---

Shaquille O'Neal found himself in an unusual situation. As a freshman at Louisiana State University, he wasn't the big wheel. The attention that year was on Chris Jackson, a six-foot-one guard out of Gulfport, Mississippi. He was the best shooting backcourtman at LSU since "Pistol Pete" Maravich in the late 1960s.

O'Neal wasn't even the tallest player on the team. Stanley Roberts, another seven-footer, was paired with O'Neal in a "Twin Towers" front court that was as impressive as any in the collegiate game. Some thought Roberts was more talented than O'Neal in certain respects.

"In Shaquille's first year, coach Dale Brown couldn't decide who was better—Shaquille or Roberts," said Charles Bennett, a sportswriter for the *New Orleans Times-Picayune.* "Stanley was more polished offensively, but Shaq had a much better work ethic. As a natural talent, Stanley had a much better shot. But Shaq worked harder and came further because of it."[1]

O'Neal still had a lot to learn: shooting free throws, for one thing, and staying out of foul trouble, for another.

"I benched him as a freshman," Brown said. "He came and sat by me maybe half a dozen games because he was fouling everybody. And he couldn't shoot. He had a bad touch. We tried to do everything possible. We worked with him every day in private drills. He was reluctant to learn new moves. He was so powerful and he could dunk the ball so easily, it was difficult to sell him anything new."[2]

Brown brought in Kareem Abdul-Jabbar and Bill Walton, two of basketball's most illustrious centers, to help O'Neal with his game. Abdul-Jabbar showed O'Neal the basic steps for the "sky hook," for which the former Los Angeles Laker center was famous. When Abdul-Jabbar shot the sky hook, a high, arcing shot, it was almost impossible to stop. Walton worked on O'Neal's all-around game, including footwork, a hook shot, and how to play defense with his hands up.

With Jackson, O'Neal, Roberts, Randy Devall, Maurice Williamson, and Vernel Singleton, the Tigers were one of Brown's most talented teams since he had begun coaching at LSU in 1972. In the sixty-four years preceding his arrival, basketball at LSU was little more than a stepchild to football. Interest in basketball ran hot and cold throughout the years, peaking during the careers of Bob Pettit (1951–54) and Pete Maravich (1968–70). Brown created new interest with his own brand of salesmanship and style. Upon his arrival, he went around the state on a mission. He called it "The Tiger Basketball Safari." Stopping wherever he saw a backyard goal, Brown introduced himself, handed out purple-and-gold basketball nets, team schedules, and business cards. In time, he changed the thinking and the face of LSU basketball.

Brown's work ethic became legendary. As an analogy, he bought a lunch pail and kept it in his office. To Brown, the lunch pail represented the blue-collar mentality that was needed to succeed in life. Hard work equals success, Brown was saying. "You cannot go to work and think that everything is going to be a banquet your whole life."[3]

Brown had twice taken LSU teams to the Final Four, the championship round of the National Collegiate Athletic Association (NCAA) playoffs. He thought the 1989–90 team was good enough to go all the way. He boastfully predicted the Tigers would "dominate the nineties." It was a prediction he would live to regret.

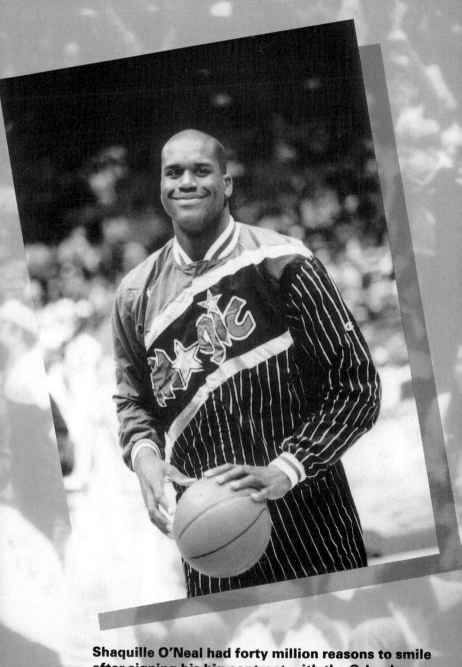

Shaquille O'Neal had forty million reasons to smile after signing his big contract with the Orlando Magic. *(Ray Stubblebine)*

Shaquille O'Neal (back row, center) was a "manageable, B-average student" in Marcia Davi
homeroom class at Fort Stewart Elementary Sche
(Marcia Davis collection)

Even in high school, Shaquille plowed over the competition "like a deer just learning to run." *(Lynne Dobson,* Austin American-Statesman*)*

Shaquille played a tall game against Hearne in the 1989 Texas state high school championships. *(Lynne Dobson,* Austin American-Statesman*)*

LSU coach Dale Brown gets a lift from a playful Shaquille O'Neal. *(Brad Messina/LSU)*

A family picture at an LSU football game: Shaquille standing with (from left) parents Phillip and Lucille Harrison, sisters Ayesha and LaTeefah, and brother Jamal. *(Brad Messina/LSU)*

In these shots at LSU, Shaquille showed he was an impressive dribbler. *(Brad Messina/LSU)*

**Shaquille believes in having a good time: Here he is
seen enjoying himself both at LSU (above) and with
a Magic teammate (right).** *(Brad Messina/LSU; Ray Stubblebi*

Shaquille and some young fans. *(Brad Messina/LSU)*

At LSU, autograph seekers never stopped coming, even during the middle of dinner. *(Brad Messina/LSU)*

The number-one pick at the NBA draft—it's Magic!
(AP/Wide World Photos)

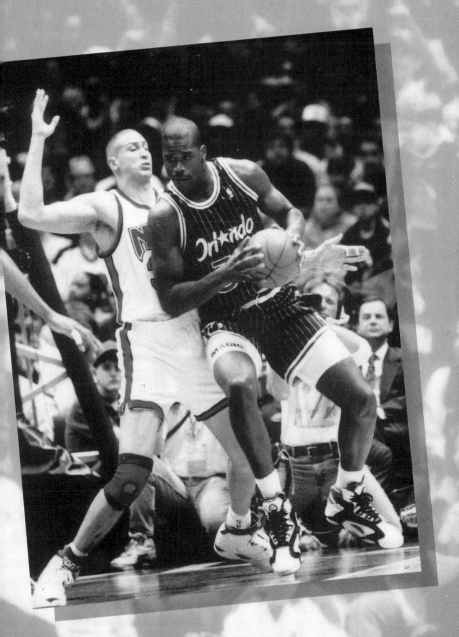

A determined Shaquille O'Neal drives to the basket against New Jersey's Sam Bowie in a game the Magic had to win—and did. *(Ray Stubblebine)*

After his powerful dunk brought down a basket at the Meadowlands in New Jersey, Shaquille had to dash to safety. Luckily, all the players walked away without injury. *(Ray Stubblebine)*

Orlando Magic coach Matt Guokas speaks—and players listen—during a time-out huddle. *(Ray Stubblebine)*

It was big news when the fans picked Shaquille O'Neal to start the NBA All-Star Game over veteran Patrick Ewing (right). Here, the seven-footers size each other up while practicing. *(AP/Wide World Photos)*

The Tigers didn't even dominate their own conference. They were a team filled with talent, but also with selfishness and petty jealousies. Said one writer: "Jackson shot too much, Stanley Roberts was too lazy, and Randy Devall wouldn't pass to anybody."[4]

Brown had named Jackson, Devall, and Wayne Sims as tri-captains. He hoped to get the right mix from a young All-American and two older players. Later in the season, Brown became so frustrated, he appointed himself team captain.

The Tigers lost to Auburn in the first round of the Southeastern Conference (SEC) playoffs. In the NCAA tournament, they beat Villanova before losing to Georgia Tech, a team that would eventually go to the Final Four. The Tigers finished with a 23–9 record and were generally regarded as underachievers.

There were some notable achievements for LSU in O'Neal's freshman year, however: a 107–105 victory over Nevada–Las Vegas, the eventual national champion, and a 148–141 overtime victory over Loyola Marymount. The game featured a classic battle between O'Neal and Loyola's Hank Gathers, resulting in a basketful of records. Not even in the days of the prolific Maravich did the Tigers score that many points in a game. It was the most points scored by a team in SEC history. "This was the most fun I have ever had in a game," Vernel Singleton said.[5]

O'Neal had fun, too. He blocked a conference-record 12 shots, scored 20 points, and grabbed 24 rebounds. Gathers, whose premature death later shocked the nation, scored 48 points. A reporter for the Associated Press wrote that the game was so quickly paced, "the official play-by-play type-writer burned out in the first half trying to keep up."

With that game, O'Neal started to come into his own. By the end of the season, he led the SEC in rebounds and blocked shots. He became the first player in conference history to block as many as 100 shots in a season. It was only a hint of things to come.

10 STANDING ALONE

''You needed the entire police force, it seemed, to get Shaquille back to the bus after the games. He was like a rock star. People wanted to touch him and wanted to get his autograph.'' —Kent Lowe, LSU associate sports information director

Shaquille O'Neal strolled through the New Orleans airport wearing his "disguise," a Phantom of the Opera mask he had picked up in the gift shop.

"What's going on, Shaquille?" LSU coach Dale Brown asked.

O'Neal held a finger to his lips.

"Coach," he said, "I don't want anyone to recognize me."[1]

Brown laughed.

With or without the mask, Shaquille O'Neal was hard to miss during the 1990–91 college basket-ball season. The most recognizable college basketball player in the country, he had drawn attention to himself with dynamic play in his sophomore year.

As a freshman, O'Neal was an agile defensive specialist and shot blocker, but he wasn't the best player at LSU. As a sophomore, however, he had become an offensive force as well, and was widely regarded as the best college player in the country. "I've never coached a gifted athlete who had improved as much from one year to the next," Brown said. "I was shocked."[2] No fewer than four organizations, including the Associated Press, named O'Neal college basketball Player of the Year his sophomore year. He also was the World Amateur Athlete of the Year, as cited by the Tanqueray company.

Unlike during his freshman year, O'Neal could now totally dominate and influence a basketball game. He had his "coming out" party on national television in a 92–82 victory over Arizona, the second-ranked team in the country. Arizona, undefeated in its first seven games, boasted a front line supposedly second to none. But it was second to O'Neal that day.

LSU, ranked number eighteen and not as highly regarded as Arizona, had something to prove. And so did O'Neal. He was coming off a freshman season that was a learning experience. He showed Arizona he was a force by scoring 29 points, grabbing 14 rebounds, and blocking 6 shots. O'Neal put the finishing touches on his performance with a ferocious dunk shot, which he followed with an impromptu dance that he called the "Shaq-de-Shaq." The fans at the Peter Maravich Assembly Center went crazy. LSU got a boost in the national rankings and O'Neal got a boost for his image.

"That put him into the public consciousness," said Lee Feinswog of the *Baton Rouge Advocate*. "National audiences now understood how dominant the kid could be. We were used to it locally."[3]

O'Neal's strong performance in the Arizona game was only the beginning. He followed with a career-high 53 points and 19 rebounds against Arkansas State . . . 29 points, 14 rebounds against Loyola-Marymount . . . 28 points, 12 rebounds, and 7 blocked shots against Illinois . . . 24 points and 20 rebounds against Nicholls State . . . 34 points and 11 rebounds against Vanderbilt . . . 28 points and 17 rebounds against Kentucky . . . and 34 points, 16 rebounds, and 7 blocked shots against Georgia.

"Shaquille runs the floor so well," Kentucky coach Rick Pitino said after a 107–88 loss to LSU later in the season. O'Neal had 33 points, 16 rebounds, and 7 blocked shots in that game. "He will probably be more dominating than [NBA stars] David Robinson and Patrick Ewing."[4]

College coaches found O'Neal nearly impossible to stop. Even when he didn't score much, which was rare, O'Neal's presence was felt. Coaches altered their game plans to play their "Shaquille O'Neal Defense." They put so much emphasis on the LSU center that they left other Tiger players open for easy baskets.

"It was no use trying to defend O'Neal," said Ed Murphy, whose Mississippi teams lost all six games to LSU in the three years he faced O'Neal. "You had to foul him out; otherwise he would win the game by himself. When you did go after him, you left other people open. When they made baskets, you lost."[5]

Murphy's first glimpse of O'Neal was enough to inspire awe and dread—he knew he would be facing this precocious man-child for some time to come. He saw O'Neal fire a long shot. The ball bounced against the plate behind the rim and back out toward the free throw line. In one swoop, O'Neal came in, caught the ball three feet in front of the basket, and dunked it. "I don't think I had ever seen anybody do that," Murphy said.

And Murphy had seen some fine players in his time, including the great Kareem Abdul-Jabbar when he was known as Lew Alcindor in the 1960s. The seven-foot Jabbar was the star center of the strong UCLA teams Murphy had gone up against when he was an assistant coach at New Mexico State. At that time, the dunk shot was not legal in college ball, but Jabbar didn't need it.

"Jabbar had a phenomenal touch; that was the first thing you noticed about him," Murphy said. "Nobody that size before or since has shot the ball like he shot it. But there was absolutely no comparison with O'Neal as far as physical size and strength. O'Neal was much stronger and fiercer on the boards."[6]

At the age of eighteen, the gifted O'Neal seemed to possess all the best qualities of other great centers before him: the athleticism of Jabbar, the physical strength of Wilt Chamberlain, and the shot-blocking and rebounding capabilities of Bill Russell. They had all dominated their sport at one time or another. Now O'Neal was on his way, part of a new breed of centers—seven-footers who could pass and dribble as well as score, rebound, and block shots.

No better example of O'Neal's multiple skills could be found than in two specific plays during his sophomore year. Against Auburn, O'Neal looked more like a guard than a center. He led LSU on a fast break, dribbling behind his back and passing off to teammate Mike Hansen for an easy layup. Traditionally in basketball, smaller players handle the ball in fast-break situations because big players, especially centers, are usually too awkward.

Against Alabama, O'Neal set up a teammate with another remarkable play. With his back to the basket, O'Neal threw an over-the-head blind pass to Vernel Singleton for a dunk, rather than turn and take a ten-foot shot himself. "Common sense will tell anybody that if you have two people under the basket, one of them is going to be open," O'Neal said. "I gave him the cut sign, and he cut, and I got it to him for the dunk. It made him look good, getting the dunk, and it made me look good."[7]

Sometimes O'Neal could look bad, too. After all, he was just eighteen years old and growing into his game. In that same Auburn game, he turned the ball over nine times.

A challenge from Brown had inspired O'Neal to take his game to the next level. Stanley Roberts, the other half of the "Twin Towers" combination in O'Neal's freshman year, had become academically ineligible to play. Chris Jackson, the gifted shooter of the 1989–90 team, had turned pro.

After O'Neal's freshman season, Brown had called him into his office.

"Shaquille, your role is going to have to change if we're going to have a chance," Brown said. He paused. "I hate to put pressure on you—I know you're only eighteen years old—but we're going to you. If we're going back to the NCAA tournament, you have to be the man."[8]

O'Neal adjusted. He raised his scoring average from 13.9 points per game to 27.6, his rebound average from 12.0 to a nation-leading 14.7, and his overall blocked shots from 115 to 140, third best in the country. There was another statistic that isn't computed: the number of missed shots that O'Neal caused because of his intimidating presence under the basket.

Now the national press was taking notice. Every top basketball writer in the country visited Baton Rouge, a little bayou town about eighty miles north of New Orleans. Photographers from national magazines followed O'Neal around—even into classrooms. O'Neal felt as if he were living in a goldfish bowl. He was besieged by crowds, autograph seekers, and admirers wherever he went. "Win or lose, people were always around Shaquille," said Kent Lowe, the LSU associate sports information director for basketball, ". . . to have his autograph, touch him, or just say hello."[9]

O'Neal, like the popular Chris Jackson before him, usually accommodated.

"We'd play at Alabama, and there would be more people waiting around the LSU dressing room when the game was over than Alabama's," recalled Jim Hawthorne, the LSU play-by-play announcer. "They were all there to see Shaquille."[10]

And Shaquille was there to be seen. He loved the attention and mixed well with people. A natural crowd pleaser, he often wore a cap with the notation "I am The Shaq-nificent." He spoke in "Shaq talk." He had names for everything, including his frontcourt teammates. "The Dunk Mob," he called them. The license plate on his car read: "33 The Deal." That was for his uniform number and "Shaquille The Deal," one of his many self-appointed nicknames that could be interpreted to stand for both his basketball and card-playing abilities.

O'Neal's following came in all sizes and shapes. Mostly, his fans were just basketball "junkies" who appreciated his unusual talents and would travel anywhere to see him. Scooter Hobbs, a reporter from Louisiana who was covering O'Neal in the NCAA playoffs that year, was in a bar in Minneapolis when a group of people walked in. Hobbs asked where they were from.

"North Dakota" was the answer. They had made the twelve-hour trip just to see O'Neal play.

In the Southeastern Conference, you could always tell when LSU was in town. The arena was usually sold out, thanks to O'Neal.

One game in South Carolina demonstrated his drawing power. The Gamecocks had lost seven straight and were in last place, yet they had the earliest home sellout in nine years. The fans came to see O'Neal, and he gave them a show. The Tigers had a big lead in the first half when O'Neal blocked a South Carolina shot. Dozens of South Carolina fans stood up and gave each other the high-five handslap. Brown thought to himself: The game's over with the crowd. Now they're looking for entertainment. The fans stayed throughout, although their team was losing by as many as 27 points at one stage. The fans didn't start heading for the exits until O'Neal left the game.

"I've never seen a crowd change its allegiance so fast," Brown said. "They were just enjoying Shaquille."[11]

O'Neal's presence demanded extra security. An off-duty state policeman traveled with the Tigers on road trips. At the NCAA playoffs in Boise, Idaho, 12,000 fans showed up to watch LSU practice. Many of them waited outside afterward, hoping to catch a glimpse of O'Neal. What should have been an easy walk through the park turned into a harrowing experience for Shaquille. As he made his way to the bus he was besieged by a frenzied mob. They all wanted a piece of him.

At LSU, O'Neal received as much mail as a rock star. Letters constantly flowed into the LSU basketball office, asking O'Neal for autographs. Fans stopped by with basketballs for him to sign.

There were few athletes busier than O'Neal at LSU, but somehow he managed to find time for young people. Once he went to an elementary school with LSU staff photographer Brad Messina to take pictures for a national magazine story.

"Shaq let each kid come up and sit on his lap, sort of like Santa Claus," Messina said. "He always wanted to make sure the kids were taken care of."[12]

O'Neal was just as aware of his responsibilities to the media. He would always come out and talk. He spiced his interviews with a sense of humor and a deep-voiced grumble that was accompanied by a wink and a smile. He delighted in kidding around with reporters.

Depending on his mood, an interview might go like this:

"How would you rate your performance tonight?"

"Sixty-eight point seven percent."

"How did the team play?"

"Seventy-one point three," said a smiling O'Neal.

Rating performances in terms of fractions of

percentages was a put-on, of course. O'Neal got a big kick out of it. Reporters who knew him got a big laugh. Reporters who didn't got an answer, even if it wasn't quite what they expected. On or off the court, O'Neal usually did the unexpected.

If O'Neal was having childish fun at the expense of others, it was usually good-natured. At times, O'Neal revealed the child inside the man's body. His fondness for pranks never ended. O'Neal and some other players were flying to a media press day for the Southeastern Conference. Vernel Singleton had accidentally spilled a box of donuts on the floor of the plane. Shaquille carefully picked them up and put them neatly back in the box. He offered the soiled donuts to Herb Vincent, the LSU sports information director. "Vincent innocently ate them," reporter Charles Bennett said. "Shaq got such a kick out of that. He laughed and laughed."[13] On many of those same plane trips, O'Neal could also be seen studying his class work.

Brown knows all about O'Neal's playful side. After O'Neal left LSU, he came back for a football game against Texas A&M.

"I was sitting up in the VIP box," Brown said, "and I didn't see him come in through the door. All of a sudden, I felt myself picked up, like you carry a woman over a threshold, and I got a big kiss on my cheek. Shaq said, 'I love you, Coach.' He's a joker."[14]

He was also a fighter, if need be. During a showdown between LSU football and basketball players, O'Neal was in the middle throwing punches.

The argument had been over a girl. O'Neal was loyal to his friends.

Otherwise, O'Neal was generally regarded as a jolly giant on campus. At LSU, O'Neal bounced through life to the beat of his own drum—or in this case, the beat of his own music. O'Neal's dormitory room was usually filled with energy, company, and lots of song. The room featured fuzzy dice hanging in the doorway, NBA All-Star posters on the wall, and an array of turntables and speakers. The musically inclined O'Neal loved to sing. He had the equipment necessary to mix his precious rap music and make his own records.

Also in O'Neal's room was a fake plastic telephone. It was a private joke. He loved to pretend he was a big shot making big-money deals on the phone. "The image in college athletics is that the star players get paid off," Brown said. "He was just mocking the system."[15]

Truth was, O'Neal never wanted anything out of LSU but a good education and the opportunity to play basketball. And no college player did it better in the 1990–91 season.

11 EYE OF THE TIGER

''They'd beat the hell out of him all the time, and referees would actually tell him, 'You're big enough—quit crying about it.' He was just really manhandled and people didn't want to hear about it because he was three hundred pounds.'' —LSU coach Dale Brown on the physical abuse suffered by Shaquille O'Neal in college games

Shaquille O'Neal was furious. The anger had been building for some time, but escalated into violence in the 1992 Southeastern Conference playoffs in Birmingham, Alabama.

O'Neal went up for a dunk shot against Tennessee. He was grabbed and hauled backward by the Volunteers' Carlus Groves.

"What are you doing, man?" O'Neal snapped,

twisting out of Groves's grasp. O'Neal swung at Groves, who was quickly pulled away. The referees forcibly separated the two. That should have been the end of it, but the fury of the two teams exploded. Both benches emptied onto the court, including Louisiana State coach Dale Brown. He made a beeline for Groves. He pushed him, screaming at him for blatantly fouling his star center.

Groves, in defense, extended his left arm in the direction of Brown's face. He missed.

Brown reached over Groves's extended arm with a right of his own. He also missed.

The others didn't. Fights broke out all over the court.

Watching the melee before them, including the emotionally crazed Brown, someone joked on press row: "Get the net!"

Order was finally restored after twenty minutes. O'Neal and Groves were ejected from the game, along with four players from each team.

The fight took the joy out of LSU's 99–89 victory. O'Neal was suspended for one game. Brown, meanwhile, received only a reprimand from the league for his behavior. Many thought he got off too easy.

A newspaper columnist from Knight-Ridder News Service said Brown should be fired. His actions compared to those of Ohio State football coach Woody Hayes, who was fired for punching a Clemson football player during the 1978 Gator Bowl.

A *Sporting News* editorial said: "Brown thought it acceptable to physically attack an opposing player. Instead of trying to restore calm, Brown added to the chaos of the moment."[1]

Brown defended his action. He went after Groves "because I saw him coming back at Shaquille. I felt our players would not get involved. I went over to restrain him, which the rules say you can do."[2]

It wasn't the first time Brown's trigger temper had gotten him in trouble. Nor the first time he and O'Neal had been involved in a violent incident. Earlier that season, police rushed to break up a brawl on the LSU campus between the football and basketball players. O'Neal was in the middle of the brawl.

When an LSU police officer pursued her investigation of the incident, she encountered resistance from Brown. He threatened to have the woman fired. He said he would "knock the hell out of her" if she were a man, according to police reports.[3] Brown apologized the following day and only received a reprimand.

The football player who had battled with O'Neal refused to press charges and the matter was dropped. Shawn King, an LSU linebacker, was upset. "I knew they weren't going to do anything," he said. "You know, everybody looks at Shaquille like he's Mister LSU."[4]

The incident at the SEC tournament in Birmingham did not win any friends for LSU. It did less to help the Tigers win games. And with O'Neal out, LSU lost to Kentucky 80–74 in the SEC semi-finals.

The loss didn't bother Brown as much as the punishment O'Neal had been taking from opposing players. Brown put together a video of what he thought was flagrant abuse of O'Neal in the 1990–91 season. He sent it to John Guthrie, the SEC's supervisor of officials. "Elbows, holding, shoving," Brown said. "I hate to sound like a crybaby. But there is so much violent play going on, he's taking a terrific beating."[5]

Not that O'Neal was an angel. "O'Neal is 7–1, about 300 pounds," the *Sporting News* pointed out. "To think O'Neal hasn't dished out his share of Shaq Hacks is silly. He plays a physical game and often gets one in return."[6] And, according to some coaches, O'Neal got his share of favorable calls from SEC referees.

The incident at Birmingham raised the level of consciousness about the problem of physical abuse in college basketball. It also made O'Neal think twice about his future.

O'Neal's father had said his son's safety would be a factor in his decision to turn pro before his college class graduated. O'Neal had one more year of eligibility at LSU but could renounce his final season by way of the NBA's early-entry rule. Under the rule, O'Neal could turn pro as long as he gave the NBA written notice within forty-five days of the college draft.

Brown recommended that Shaquille forgo his final year and turn professional, rather than risk

being injured by an intentional foul. As Brown ex-
plained, "If they want to drive him to the NBA, I
guess this embarrassment at the SEC tournament
in Birmingham might be the last straw."[7]

Despite his emotional reaction at the tournament, Brown's heart was in the right place. He
was trying to protect his player. "Players are like
your sons after a while," Brown said.[8]

It was O'Neal's real father, however, who would
have the greatest input into his son's decision. But
first, LSU had to play more basketball—the NCAA
tournament.

12 GOING IN STYLE

''He's such a force, he's scary. When he got the ball inside, you couldn't stop him.'' —Indiana's Calbert Cheaney after facing Shaquille O'Neal in the 1992 NCAA playoffs

B oise, Idaho, was a million miles from Baton Rouge. Or so it seemed to the LSU basketball team. For Shaquille O'Neal, it might be the end of the road. Was Boise where he would play his last game for LSU? Nobody knew for sure, and O'Neal wasn't saying.

While people were wondering about his future, O'Neal was only thinking about the first round of the NCAA playoffs. Brigham Young University was a worrisome opponent. The BYU Cougars came into the playoffs with confidence and mo-

mentum after winning the Western Athletic Conference tournament.

The change of scene was a welcome relief to
LSU after the highly publicized violence in the
SEC tournament. In Boise, no one seemed to care
about the incident in Birmingham. It was ancient
history. Every basketball fan who was lucky to
have a tournament ticket was anxious to see LSU
and its heralded center in action. O'Neal, for one,
was just glad to be back after his one-game suspension.

"Going to Boise was the best thing that could
have happened to our team," said LSU associate
sports information director Kent Lowe. "It took
the incident in Birmingham out of the limelight.
It didn't seem to matter much to the media or the
people watching the game."[1]

LSU coach Dale Brown was concerned about
O'Neal's penchant for fouls. Brown needn't have
worried. O'Neal gave a memorable performance:
26 points, 13 rebounds, and an NCAA-record 11
blocked shots as LSU beat BYU 94–83.

The Cougars had no answers for O'Neal. "He
blocked a lot of shots," said BYU coach Roger
Reid. "It's intimidating in there. We're not
ashamed to lose to that basketball team because
O'Neal is the best basketball player in America."[2]

Indiana coach Bobby Knight thought so, too.
He called O'Neal "the most effective center since
Bill Walton,"[3] the UCLA great who led the Bruins
to two national championships in the 1970s.

Knight had no way of stopping O'Neal either.

But he did find a way to stop LSU. Against Indiana, O'Neal was powerful with 36 points, 12 rebounds, and 5 blocked shots. It wasn't enough. With fifty-three seconds left, O'Neal walked off the court at Boise State Pavilion to a thunderous standing ovation. He got a hug and a kiss from Brown, sat down on the bench, and wiped tears from his eyes as he watched the final moments of an 89–79 loss to the Hoosiers.

O'Neal's performance was one of the few positives Brown could bring away from that loss. It was especially grating to lose to Knight, an old adversary. Brown had always regarded Knight as a bully. He was appalled in 1981 when the Indiana coach stuffed a taunting LSU fan into a garbage can. Tensions between the two coaches intensified during an NCAA playoff game in 1987 when Knight threw one of his more memorable tantrums. He stormed over to the scorer's table to dispute a call against his team. His fists slammed the table and a phone went flying into the air in front of the startled officials. The incident ignited the Hoosiers to a victory over LSU.

If Brown was not a fan of Knight's, the feeling was mutual. Knight had taken every opportunity to disparage Brown's coaching abilities. He once remarked, "I was worried about losing until I looked down the floor and saw Dale Brown. Then I knew we had a chance."[4]

Brown couldn't be blamed for this loss: Outside of O'Neal, LSU had a poor shooting night. Indiana, however, had a good one. Still, the Tigers managed to stay closer than they had the year before, when they had lost by 17 points to Connecticut in the first round of the NCAAs.

O'Neal's big performances against BYU and Indiana were indicative of his junior year. Although statistically he did not match his Player of the Year season as a sophomore, his scoring and rebounding were among the nation's best. But not even his great performances could lift a troubled team. Despite O'Neal's greatness, and probably because of it, there were petty jealousies among his teammates. Everything revolved around O'Neal. Keeping him happy, it seemed, was Brown's most important coaching assignment. But he couldn't keep everyone happy. "O'Neal's teammates learned to hold back," one writer observed, "but the Tigers still led the nation in friction."[5]

If O'Neal had any regrets about his junior season, the Birmingham brawl would be number one. Right behind might be an incident involving David Duke, the former Grand Wizard of the Ku Klux Klan who was running for governor in Louisiana. One thing about O'Neal, he was always lively material for the media, whether fighting or talking.

Reporter Scooter Hobbs of Louisiana's *Lake Charles American Press* was interviewing members of the LSU basketball team for a story about Duke for governor. When he asked O'Neal for a reaction to the Duke candidacy, the player said, "I try not to worry about that kind of stuff."[6]

The innocent remark was misinterpreted to mean Shaquille didn't mind if Duke was governor. Soon it became a national issue, a black man apparently supporting a KKK member for governor.

Brown's reaction was predictable.

"Brown went crazy," Hobbs said. "He wanted to know what Shaquille had said."[7]

Soon, O'Neal corrected himself—and corrected Duke. In a public statement, he called Duke a "liar."

"I resent it totally. I want the fans and the people in the community to know I'm no Uncle Tom [a disparaging name given a black man for passively catering to whites]."[8]

All this was just about forgotten by the end of the season. Now O'Neal would be making a different kind of statement. Would he remain at LSU for his final year of eligibility, or turn pro?

The sports world waited.

13 MAKING A DECISION

"Everyone has been dying for O'Neal to get out. He's that good right now." —Cleveland Cavaliers scout Bill McKinney in anticipation of Shaquille O'Neal leaving college for the National Basketball Association

*T*he Cole High School gymnasium in San Antonio, Texas, bustled with activity. Television lights flooded the tiny gym, jammed with media and friends and family of Shaquille O'Neal.

Everyone was there for the press conference called by O'Neal, presumably to announce his decision to turn pro. It had stirred nationwide interest. The broadcast was beamed back to Louisiana State University, where many watched with anticipation.

Dressed in a suit, O'Neal sat at a long table in front of several microphones and tape recorders. He was flanked by his parents, sisters LaTeefah and Ayesha, and brother Jamal. Radio and television reporters pressed forward in a tangle of wires, eagerly awaiting O'Neal's words. The conference began . . .

Less than a week before, O'Neal had met with LSU basketball coach Dale Brown to discuss his (O'Neal's) future. Brown's feelings were well known. He had urged O'Neal to turn pro.

"It just wasn't as much fun as it should have been for him," Brown said of O'Neal's junior season. "The college game was no longer for him. People were always trying to hurt him."[1]

Brown had complained constantly that O'Neal had been abused by opposing teams. Brown feared for the safety of his star player. If he was going to take a pounding, Brown thought, he might as well be paid for it.

O'Neal was troubled by the physical abuse he took playing college basketball. The hard foul that led to the brawl in the SEC tournament seemed to be the last straw. "I'm not making this decision out of anger or frustration, but everyone who saw the SEC tournament knows that an injustice was done,"[2] said O'Neal, referring to his one-game suspension for the incident. Besides, O'Neal wanted to be remembered for his basketball-playing ability at LSU, not for brawling.

O'Neal could have easily turned pro at the end of his sophomore year and signed a huge contract.

"It surprised me that he stayed his junior year, although I was delighted that he did," said LSU athletic director Joe Dean.[3]

O'Neal's parents were influential in his decision to stay in school. They wanted him to be the first in the family to get a college degree.

O'Neal's press conference had caught the LSU basketball public relations staff off guard. On April 1, Kent Lowe received a phone call. Brown, in Minneapolis for the NCAA basketball tournament, had received a fax stating O'Neal was holding a press conference at Fort Sam Houston. Lowe's first thought: April Fool!

It was no joke. Lowe and a group of local writers rushed to the press conference. It was not a happy trip for some of the writers. They thought O'Neal snubbed LSU by not having the conference on campus.

At one o'clock, a hush fell over the crowd at the Cole gymnasium as the press conference began. O'Neal made the announcement everyone expected: He was leaving LSU for the pros.

"I feel that in my heart, it's time for a change and it's time for me to move on," he said. "I said to myself, 'Am I having fun?' And I reviewed in my mind this past season. I wasn't having that much fun."

O'Neal paused.

"I was told at an early age, if it's not fun, do something else."[4]

O'Neal's announcement didn't surprise anyone in the National Basketball Association, where he would be the prize catch in that summer's draft. Some NBA executives figured O'Neal would command the biggest salary ever given to a rookie. Other good players were available in that year's draft, among them Duke University's Christian Laettner. Laettner was the college player of the year, but everyone knew who would be the number-one pick.

Everyone but O'Neal, it seemed.

"I don't know," O'Neal said, when asked if he thought he was going to be number one. "Sometimes the best player doesn't go as the first pick."[5]

14 HITTING THE SHAQPOT

''There were eleven guys sitting there with Shaq uniforms. So whoever came out of there with the winning ball was going to unveil their jersey. Obviously, he was going to be the pick.''
—Orlando Magic president and general manager Pat Williams talking about the National Basketball Association draft lottery of 1992

It was Lottery Day in the National Basketball Association. The future of eleven teams was in an envelope. One of them was going to have the number-one pick in the 1992 draft.

There were several great prospects, but no question who would be number one: Shaquille O'Neal literally and figuratively stood head and shoulders above them all. He was the best draft prospect, pro scouts proclaimed, since Patrick Ewing in 1985. They called O'Neal a "franchise player" whose single-handed impact could dramatically affect the fortunes of a team. He would be a signature player for years to come.

NBA commissioner David Stern had started opening the envelopes that would reveal the order of draft picks for the eligible teams. Under NBA rules, a team is eligible for the lottery if it finished out of the playoffs the previous season.

The actual lottery is conducted in secrecy rivaling any high-level government meeting, and it is supervised by a major accounting firm. Ping-Pong balls with the team logos fill an air-popping device, similar to ones used in state lotteries. The team with the poorest record has the best odds, with eleven balls. The team with the best record has the poorest odds, with only one ball of the sixty-six. The teams having the first three selections are determined by the air-popping balls. The eight teams that are left are then assigned spots in inverse order of their records, the team with the worst going first. The results of the lottery are placed in envelopes, which are opened on lottery day in Academy Awards–fashion by Stern.

Pat Williams, president and general manager of the Magic, was understandably nervous sitting on the NBA entertainment studio stage with the rest of the team officials in Secaucus, New Jersey. The

Magic, an NBA expansion team, had completed their third year in the league with disastrous results.

Williams, who wore a championship ring as general manager of the Philadelphia 76ers, was starting at the bottom in Orlando. He was trying to build a new team from scratch, and it showed. The records were 18–64, 31–51, and 21–61 in his first three years.

The Magic's first draft pick in franchise history, in 1989, was Nick Anderson, a six-foot-six forward from the University of Illinois. Anderson would lead the team in scoring by his third season, but he was not considered a franchise player.

When Stern opened another envelope and announced, "Dallas Mavericks," Williams realized he was closer to his goal. Since the choices are announced in inverse order, last to first, Williams knew he was among the final three picks. His palms began to sweat.

Stern opened another envelope.

"Minnesota Timberwolves," he said.

Now the Magic was in the final two.

Williams squirmed in his seat. This was pressure—something he was familiar with. He had become general manager of the 76ers in 1974, and it had taken him nine years to build a championship team.

One more envelope and Shaq is ours! Williams thought.

As Stern walked across the stage and picked up the envelope, Williams's heart picked up a beat.

Stern tore open the fateful envelope with a dramatic flair and smiled.

"The second pick in the 1992 NBA draft," Stern said, "belongs to . . . the Charlotte Hornets!"

For the first time in his life, Williams was speechless. Known as a tireless talker who always had something bright and funny to say, Williams at that moment "went blank."

The Magic won the number-one pick! They had the rights to Shaquille O'Neal!

"I knew I was supposed to have some reaction," Williams said, "but I was so numb, I didn't know what to do. I had been so focused on Charlotte winning again [the Hornets had the first pick in the NBA lottery in 1991]. It didn't register that we'd won."[1]

Just minutes after Stern placed Orlando's card beside the number-one pick, the phone began ringing at the Magic ticket office. Fans were already seeking season tickets. Fifty were sold that night, and another 150 in the next twenty-four hours. Soon, callers were greeted by the song "Love Shack" by the rock group the B-52s when they dialed the office. The Magic formally drafted O'Neal on June 24, 1992.

"We were not entertaining any offers for Shaquille," Williams said. "A guy like that comes along once in a lifetime, so there was no debating, no interviews. He was going to be the pick from minute one. Every other club was going to do the same thing."[2]

Williams still faced the hardest part of his job:

signing O'Neal to a contract keeping the Magic under the NBA salary cap. Under NBA regulations, teams must stay under a total maximum salary figure for their players. In this era of spiraling salaries, the cap helps prevent the financial collapse of teams.

"That was the hardest part," Williams said. "The lottery was easy. All we did was sit and sweat. On the cap, we had lawyers, accountants, financial experts, the league people. It was enormously complicated and intense."[3]

If anyone was familiar with "complicated and intense," it was Williams. He and his wife, Jill, have sixteen children—four biological and twelve adopted. But not even eighteen people living in one house presented the kind of problems facing Williams. He had to figure a way to restructure several of the players' contracts in order to get O'Neal under the cap.

With the help of some of the Magic players, he managed to do it. They redesigned their contracts so O'Neal could bring his forceful talents to Orlando. The Magic restructured five contracts, traded one player who wouldn't go along, and gave up their rights to another. From start to finish, it took fifteen days. "I don't think any club will ever have to do that again," said Williams,[4] who had little sleep during the negotiations. Finally, a seven-year deal worth about $40 million was struck for O'Neal with Los Angeles agent Leonard Armato, whose clients included former great Kareem Abdul-Jabbar.

"We found him to be very fair and realistic,"

Williams said of Armato. "Obviously it was a big number, and I'm sure he was satisfied. But he could have killed this whole thing—he could have waited. I just think everybody did what had to be done. Truly, it was a team effort."[5]

15 SUDDEN IMPACT

''He's a fun-loving kid off the court, but on the court he's already a man. He already has shown me a great deal of maturity. He looks like he loves to play this game.'' —Orlando Magic coach Matt Guokas upon first seeing Shaquille O'Neal

I t was only the first month of the NBA season, but the atmosphere at Madison Square Garden in New York had the feeling of playoff hysteria. Ticket scalpers mingled with the surging crowd. Noise and excitement filled the building known as the "world's greatest arena." Celebrities such as actor Peter Falk, moviemaker Spike Lee, and former basketball great Wilt Chamberlain added a glamorous touch to the occasion.

Normally an NBA game in November, even one

in the Garden, would not generate such a response. But this night was special. Shaquille O'Neal was in town with the Orlando Magic, and his anticipated battle with New York Knicks center Patrick Ewing was one of the biggest sports events of the season.

Like a heavyweight fight, a battle of behemoths in the NBA was a big drawing card. It was power against power, and in this case O'Neal's first real test against a top professional center. Ewing, like O'Neal, had been a number-one pick in the NBA draft. Now O'Neal would challenge him in a head-to-head duel at center court. It was a match made in marketing heaven: the established star center against the young challenger.

This battle of goliaths was a link to the NBA's golden past, when centers were usually the main attraction. In recent years, the focus had largely shifted to smaller players with astounding athletic talents, such as Magic Johnson, Larry Bird, and Michael Jordan. It had been a long time since the memorable clashes between Wilt Chamberlain and Bill Russell. Those two staged some of the greatest personal duels in NBA history. The last came in 1969, three years before O'Neal was born. Chamberlain, who played in Philadelphia, San Francisco, and Los Angeles, usually won the scoring titles; Russell's Boston Celtics usually won the team championships.

Later, Chamberlain faced Kareem Abdul-Jabbar and Willis Reed in high-profile duels. And

Abdul-Jabbar waged tremendous battles with Reed and Nate Thurmond.

Among the centers in the NBA in the nineties, Ewing was considered to be in a special class, along with Houston's Hakeem Olajuwon and San Antonio's David Robinson. Ewing had been a six-time All-Star and was one of the most respected big men in the game.

O'Neal, despite having played only a few games, was already being mentioned in the same breath with other past greats. Because of his strength and power, the seven-foot-one, 300-pound O'Neal was mostly compared to Chamberlain, a seven-foot-one, 255-pound rookie in the 1959–60 season.

Ewing was hyped to a certain degree when he came into the NBA in 1985, but it couldn't compare to the hype and marketing attention O'Neal received as a rookie. O'Neal was featured in a national TV commercial for the Reebok sneaker company. His status was evident by the stars who appeared with him: Chamberlain, Jabbar, Russell, and Bill Walton. In the commercial, O'Neal is put to the "test" by the former great centers to see if he really has what it takes to succeed in the NBA.

"Show us how you dunk, Shaquille." One of them hands him the ball.

He goes up and smashes it through the hoop, shattering the glass backboard into countless pieces.

O'Neal is smug. He turns and looks to the others for approval. He gets none. Instead, he gets a broom and dustpan—to clean up the mess he has made.

The commercial fades out. O'Neal's voice-over lingers.

"Oh, this must be a rookie thing," he says, dismayed.

In real life, though, it was hard to knock the smile off O'Neal's face. And why not? He was getting paid the richest contract in basketball to play a game he loved. And he loved the pro game even more than college.

"In college they wouldn't let me do anything," he said. "When I would post up a guy, he would throw down a little Marlon Brando act and referees would make the call against me. Up here, the players are more my size, and they let you play more physically."[1]

There were times, however, when the pro game tested O'Neal's patience and his temper. Later that season, he created headlines by punching Detroit's Alvin Robertson, a half foot shorter, during a game shown on national television. The incident occurred after O'Neal was deliberately fouled by Detroit's Bill Laimbeer and the two confronted each other. Robertson claimed he was just trying to be a peacemaker; O'Neal claimed Robertson hit him below the belt out of camera range, and his punch was retaliatory.

O'Neal was thrown out, fined $10,250, and suspended for one game. The loss of the game amounted to an additional $36,585 loss in salary.

It was a big story in the NBA, particularly with

a recent explosion of on-court violence. Just two weeks earlier, the New York Knicks and Phoenix Suns were in a brawl resulting in the suspension of three players and nearly $300,000 in fines.

O'Neal was being well paid to take a beating under the basket. He made nearly $6 million a year. By comparison, Chamberlain made $65,000 in his rookie year.

Media demand for O'Neal was overwhelming. The Magic publicity department scheduled special Shaquille O'Neal press conferences in cities the team was visiting for the first time. During a visit to Los Angeles, Magic publicist Alex Martins counted at least sixty-five media people and ten TV cameras. After a while, the Magic had to limit O'Neal's media accessibility. The team was getting as many as thirty to forty requests a day for interviews.

The Magic could not control the crowds as easily. Martins had to run interference for O'Neal after an exhibition game in Asheville, North Carolina. It took fifteen minutes to clear a fifteen-foot path. "I got the feeling I was clearing the way for the Beatles," Martins said.[2]

On the road, the Magic routinely found 100 to 200 fans waiting at hotels. One night, the team bus pulled up to a hotel in Chicago at 2:30 A.M. The players were surprised. The area seemed deserted. When O'Neal stepped off the bus, dozens of fans suddenly appeared out of nowhere and swamped the Orlando center. Because it was so cold, they had been sitting in their cars.

The Magic did their best to protect O'Neal from abuse by crowds. It was enough that he had to take punishment on the court. When the Magic played at home, O'Neal had valet parking and was escorted in and out of the arena by a security guard.

O'Neal had become one of the world's most popular athletes in a very short time. He seemed to be everywhere—on the cover of *Sports Illustrated,* on "The Arsenio Hall Show," the "Today" show, and "Entertainment Tonight." He was even the subject of a special one-hour segment on ESPN, the national sports cable network.

If all this was turning O'Neal's head, it didn't show. He was cooperative with the media and teammates. When told that Terry Catledge already had the number 33 jersey he was promised, O'Neal deferred to the veteran and took number 32 instead. "A number's not important," O'Neal said.[3]

On the court, O'Neal's enthusiasm was a joy to behold. From his first pro game, when he dribbled the length of the court and hit a dunk shot against Miami, O'Neal attracted attention. He scored 35 points in three quarters against Charlotte; had 31 points and 21 rebounds against Washington—more rebounds than the Bullets' entire starting five—and 29 points and 15 rebounds against New Jersey.

By the time the Magic played the Knicks in New York in late November, O'Neal was leading the NBA in rebounding and was fourth in scoring.

O'Neal had overpowered every other center he had played that season. But Ewing—at seven feet and 240 pounds—was a stronger test. "It was the most anticipated game that I've seen in a long time," said Barry Cooper, a sportswriter for the *Orlando Sentinel*, "and there was a buzz in the Garden."[4]

The buzz became a roar, as Knicks fans cheered their team's 92–77 victory. But although the Magic were outplayed, O'Neal held his own against Ewing and a Knicks defense that at times covered him with three players. Point-wise, O'Neal had a subpar game with 18, but he still managed to outscore Ewing by 3. He outrebounded him 17–9 as the two giants virtually nullified each other and let the Knicks' smaller players decide the game.

O'Neal's inexperience showed at times. After all, it was only his eighth professional game. Ewing was in his eighth season. O'Neal committed seven turnovers, and although he blocked some of Ewing's shots inside, he couldn't stop Ewing's jump shot. But he did show something to the Knicks' Tony Campbell.

"With his strength and zeal, he'll definitely be in the class of Abdul-Jabbar," said Campbell, who once played with the great Los Angeles Lakers center. "If not now, then soon. He's doing this on raw talent. I'd hate to see him when he learns how to play this game."[5]

16 ALL-STAR CONTRO-VERSY

"I worked hard. I deserved it. Maybe in five or six years, someone will beat me out. Good luck to them." —Shaquille O'Neal after he was selected to start in the 1993 NBA All-Star Game

Shaquille O'Neal found himself in the NBA All-Star Game, and in the middle of a controversy. The storm came after he outplayed the New York Knicks' Patrick Ewing in their second meeting.

Knicks coach Pat Riley was upset. O'Neal had been selected to start for the Eastern Conference in the All-Star Game. Riley felt Ewing should have been the choice. Riley made his feelings public, and made waves that reached Florida.

O'Neal was the clear choice of the fans who vote for All-Star players. He outpolled Ewing by nearly 250,000 votes—826,767 to 578,368—even though Magic fans got a late start in the voting. The original ballots were recalled when O'Neal's name was incorrectly spelled "O'Neill."

While All-Star games are generally popularity contests, O'Neal proved his worth in battles with some of the league's top centers. O'Neal had more than held his own against Patrick Ewing in their first meeting. In their second, O'Neal scored 22 points and blocked several shots by Ewing as the Magic beat the Atlantic Division leaders 95–94. In their third meeting, Ewing had 34 points. But he fouled out, and O'Neal scored 21 to spark the Magic to their second victory over the Knicks. Playing for the first time against Houston's Hakeem Olajuwon, O'Neal matched the Rockets' All-Star with 13 rebounds to lead a 107–94 Orlando win.

Ewing took the All-Star issue personally. Although he said publicly it didn't bother him to lose the starting assignment to a rookie, he told a Magic clubhouse attendant, "Can you believe that Shaq is beating me in the All-Star voting?"[1]

Riley couldn't believe it either.

"It's ridiculous that O'Neal is starting the All-Star Game in front of Patrick," Riley said. "You cannot compare the accomplishments of the two."[2]

Riley was a big believer in seniority. Ewing, in his eighth season, played on the NBA's "Dream

Team" that won the gold medal at the 1992 Olympics and was a starter in the All-Star Game for three straight years.

Statistically, however, O'Neal had the edge over Ewing at the All-Star break. He was second in the league in rebounding, second in blocked shots, second in field goal percentage, and seventh in scoring. And just months into his rookie season, O'Neal exceeded Ewing in fan popularity. Actually, outside of Michael Jordan, not too many players in the NBA had O'Neal's drawing power.

"I'm not an actor, but I am an entertainer," O'Neal said. "I'm happy that the fans like to see me play. I'm seven feet one, three hundred pounds. I dunk hard, I slide on the floor, I get rebounds. I can dribble the length of the court. And, hey, people want to see that. If I was a fan, I'd want to come and see Shaq play, too."[3]

O'Neal, only the fourteenth rookie in NBA history to start an All-Star Game, joined Chicago's Michael Jordan and Scottie Pippen, Detroit's Isiah Thomas, and Charlotte's Larry Johnson in the starting lineup for the Eastern Conference. San Antonio's David Robinson, Phoenix's Charles Barkley, Utah's Karl Malone and John Stockton, and Portland's Clyde Drexler were the Western Conference starters.

In the midst of those great players, O'Neal became a star attraction. Outside of Jordan, no player received as much attention from fans and media at the All-Star Game in Salt Lake City. His stature grew immeasurably when the NBA held a charity auction and O'Neal's jersey sold for $55,000—$30,000 more than Jordan's.

"That's great, they must have really wanted it," O'Neal said.[4]

The All-Star Game wasn't the only highlight of the weekend for O'Neal. He also rapped with his favorite group, Fu Schnickens. O'Neal, wearing a gold chain and a flashy rap outfit, performed "What's Up, Doc" with the group at the NBA's Stay in School Jam the day before the game.

"It's great being me," he told reporters during the All-Star weekend. "This is turning into a fun weekend."[5]

Riley, coach of the Eastern Conference All-Stars, played no favorites in the game. He tried to get equal time for everyone. O'Neal and Ewing both played twenty-five minutes, although Riley kept the Orlando center on the bench for sixteen straight minutes in the second period.

"I guess Pat Riley wanted more experience down the stretch," O'Neal said diplomatically.[6]

Said Riley: "I wanted to get everyone enough minutes and then take a look at what was going on in the fourth quarter. I wasn't counting the number of minutes people were sitting out. I was counting the number of minutes that everybody got. That was important."[7]

O'Neal made his minutes count. He started quickly, hitting three free throws. Then he sank a fifteen-footer. By halftime, O'Neal had scored 13 points in fourteen minutes. He finished with 14 points and 7 rebounds.

"It was fun just being out there, playing with all the great players," said O'Neal after the West beat the East 135–132 in overtime.[8]

O'Neal refused to be drawn into any controversy over his playing time. Besides, there was more important business ahead. He had to help the Magic make the playoffs.

17 IN THE HUNT

''I'm a lot smarter than I used to be. You know, when you win games, you're smarter.''
—Orlando Magic general manager Pat Williams following a twenty-game improvement in the 1992–93 season, best in the NBA

For a change, April in Orlando meant more than just spring break at Disney World. For the first time in the four years of their existence, the Magic were contenders for a playoff berth.

The Magic headed into the final month of the season embroiled in a crowded, frantic race for the final playoff spots in the NBA's Eastern Conference. The Charlotte Hornets and their brilliant rookie, Alonzo Mourning, were among the competing teams.

Mourning was the one player who could challenge the favored Shaquille O'Neal for Rookie of the Year honors. The former Georgetown center, the number-two pick in the draft, was having a superb year in his own right for the up-and-coming Hornets.

The Orlando-Charlotte game featured a rousing battle of the rookie stars: Mourning matched O'Neal shot for shot. At the end of three quarters, each had 21 points.

The Magic, sparked by their reserves, led 84–75. The lead dwindled to 5 points early in the fourth quarter. Then O'Neal asserted himself. He outscored Mourning 8–0 in the final twelve minutes, helping the Magic pull away to a 109–96 victory.

"Shaq had a great game," Charlotte coach Allan Bristow said after watching O'Neal score 29 points and grab 10 rebounds. "It was Shaq that set the tone for it all. When they had to have the buckets, he was the one they turned to."[1]

But with less than two weeks left in the season, the lights started to dim on the Magic. A loss to Philadelphia diminished their playoff hopes. When they lost to Cleveland, it was a dark day in Orlando. The Magic had lost two in a row.

They desperately needed to beat the Boston Celtics, who were riding a three-game winning streak. Both teams played an aggressive, hard-nosed defensive game. With thirty-two seconds remaining, Nick Anderson broke an eight-minute scoring drought for the Magic to hold off the Celtics. O'Neal scored 20 points and pulled down 21 rebounds as the Magic won 88–79. The Magic had once more tightened up the playoff race.

"I just want to tell people, don't count us out," O'Neal said.[2] There were four games to go.

"We just have to win all four, starting with Washington," O'Neal said. "We have to be careful. Anyone can lose on any given night."[3]

Against the Bullets two nights later, O'Neal had 20 points and 25 rebounds—his seventh "20-20" game—as the Magic won 105–86.

"If we win our next three games and we have forty-two wins, I'll find it hard to believe that we won't be in the playoffs," Anderson said.[4]

That optimistic note struck a sour chord, however, when the Magic went to Boston and were hammered 126–98 by the Celtics. It was a severe blow to the Magic's playoff hopes. Miraculously, though, they were still alive: The Magic had to win their last two games and hope that Indiana lost its last two.

It looked grim to the Orlando players. O'Neal was almost resigned to failure.

"I'm only twenty-one," he said. "We'll have a lot of other chances."[5]

The Magic stayed alive when they beat New Jersey 119–116, while Indiana lost to Detroit 109–104. Anderson played a remarkable game for the Magic, scoring 50 points. But, once again, O'Neal stole the headlines. He brought down his second backboard of the season, this time in the Meadowlands Arena.

Now, with one game to go, the Magic were still

breathing. They had to beat Atlanta and hope that Indiana lost to Miami.

Whatever momentum the Magic had from the New Jersey game was not apparent as they got off to a poor start against the Hawks. They fell behind 12–2. But O'Neal, their irrepressible force, led them back. O'Neal, who had been held to 10 points and 5 rebounds against New Jersey, had 11 points and 11 rebounds in the first quarter alone against Atlanta.

Orlando led 48–37 at the half. Then Anderson scored 11 points in the third quarter as the Magic went up 68–48 to put the game out of Atlanta's reach.

Final: Orlando 104, Atlanta 85.

O'Neal finished with 31 points and 18 rebounds in a brilliant performance when the Magic really needed it. They had won the game they had to win. But they still didn't know if they had won a place in the playoffs.

The Magic waited for the conclusion of the Indiana-Miami game. Many of their avid fans remained in their seats at Orlando Arena, mesmerized by the television screen.

Finally, the game ended—and so did the Magic's season. Indiana beat Miami 94–88 to clinch the final playoff berth.

Not much separated Orlando from Indiana at the end of the season. Both teams had 41–41 records. A tie-breaker system decided which team went to the playoffs. The edge went to the Pacers because they had outscored the Magic by 5 points collectively in their four meetings.

"It was tough because we had a good year," said Pat Williams, the Magic's president and general manager. "But we looked at the big picture, and it was a very significantly improved year for us."[6]

The Magic had a lot to show for the season. Their .500 record represented the best in the team's history, a twenty-game improvement over the previous season's 21–61, and the most improved record in the league.

For Shaquille O'Neal and the Magic, it was not just the end of the season. It was the beginning of a new era in Orlando.

18 ROOKIE OF THE YEAR

''I hope I can get an NBA championship trophy to go along with it, so that when I retire and have children, I can tell my son, 'I was bad.' '' —Shaquille O'Neal after winning the NBA's Rookie of the Year award

"**A**t seven feet one, three hundred and three pounds, you're supposed to go out there, dunk, rebound, and battle. I was just doing my job."[1]

With those words, Shaquille O'Neal accepted the NBA's Rookie of the Year award in the spring of 1993.

It was no surprise. O'Neal was virtually a unanimous choice by the nationwide panel of sportswriters and broadcasters who cover the NBA. He received ninety-six out of a possible ninety-eight votes. Charlotte's Alonzo Mourning received the other two.

O'Neal headed the NBA's all-rookie team for the 1992–93 season, which included Mourning, Minnesota's Christian Laettner, Washington's Tom Gugliotta, and Denver's LaPhonso Ellis.

O'Neal took the NBA by storm. In his first game, he grabbed 18 rebounds against Miami, the most for a rookie since Bill Walton in 1974. After five games, O'Neal led the NBA in rebounding, was tied for fourth in scoring, and was fifth in blocked shots—a remarkable achievement for a first-year player. While most players that age were developing, O'Neal was dominating. O'Neal's performance earned him the NBA Player of the Week award in his first week—the first time a rookie won the award at the start of the season.

The moment he stepped on the court for the Magic, O'Neal commanded respect. On the first play, in his first exhibition game, Orlando won the tap. O'Neal was immediately surrounded by three Miami players as he posted up near the basket. "That probably said it all," remembered Magic general manager Pat Williams. "Here was this kid who never played a pro game before. The first time he touches the ball, the instructions are to drop three guys on him."[2]

As a rookie, O'Neal knew he had a lot to learn.

"I figured my first year in the league, I would score maybe twelve points a game, get a half-dozen rebounds, block a couple of shots," O'Neal said.[3]

O'Neal doubled his expectations. He was the only player in the NBA to finish in the top ten in four statistical categories. He was second in the league in rebounding (13.9 per game) and shot-blocking (3.53), fourth in shooting percentage (.562 from the field), and eighth in scoring (23.4).

After O'Neal's fast start, the rookie award was believed to be his to lose. Orlando coach Matt Guokas feared the Magic's magnificent man-child, though a superb specimen, wouldn't have the physical stamina to handle the long NBA season. For most rookies, the length of the pro season is a major adjustment. Because it is three times longer than the college season, rookies can experience fatigue. In the NBA, it is referred to as "hitting the wall." But while most rookies were hitting the wall, O'Neal still had energy enough to break through it. He started and finished fast, pacing himself like a seasoned pro. "He held up very well," Williams said. "There was no down time. He never had a bad streak."[4]

O'Neal actually thrived on work. It was something that defined his life. He had grown up with a strong work ethic in a goal-oriented family. Originally, O'Neal picked up a basketball because it was something to do. He wasn't always proficient at the game. His awkwardness as a youngster was a source of merriment for insensitive playmates. He was the tallest on the playground but hardly the best. His legs were pencil-thin and he was gawky. He wasn't able to jump very high and he couldn't dunk. He was embarrassed.

But he was also motivated—partly because of his embarrassment, but mostly because of his competitive fire. Coaches at every level of O'Neal's basketball experience found him to be the hardest worker on the team.

As a thirteen-year-old, he set a goal. He enlisted Louisiana State coach Dale Brown's help for a weight program to strengthen his legs and arms. Soon, his playground buddies weren't laughing. Nor was his coach at Fulda High School in Germany. O'Neal wasn't just another big kid taking up space.

O'Neal made believers of his high school coaches back in the States. He continued to work hard. His coaches remembered he was the first to come to practice, and the last to leave. With perseverance, his strength continued to grow. He was not only dunking with a flair, he was bending rims.

At LSU, O'Neal rose to his biggest challenge. Brown called on O'Neal to "carry the team" and to take his game to another level. Accepting Brown's challenge, O'Neal worked tirelessly. In his freshman year, he was a good player. In his sophomore year, he became a dominating one.

And now, in the NBA, he was reaching for new levels. O'Neal impressed everyone on the Magic with an inquisitive nature and a passion to learn.

O'Neal's amazing raw talent overcame deficiencies in his rookie season. He committed too many fouls, made too many turnovers, and didn't make enough free throws.

"If he ever learns to make them consistently, you can forget it," said Los Angeles Lakers general manager Jerry West. "No one will want to foul him."[5]

Other than his dunk, O'Neal lacked a specialty shot. He operated on raw power. Overall, though, it was hard to fault his first season as a professional.

"You have to love his work ethic, his competitive drive, his enthusiasm for the game, and his sense for the dramatic play," said former great Bill Walton.[6]

19 THE MAGIC KINGDOM

''Someday, I'll be the man. You can underline that three times.''
—Shaquille O'Neal

Shaquille O'Neal arrived in Orlando. He stepped off the plane wearing Mickey Mouse ears and a big, lopsided grin.

"Shaqie Mouse is here," he quipped.[1]

O'Neal, it seemed, was prepared to challenge Mickey Mouse for the Magic Kingdom. He was no cartoon character. If anything, the seven-foot-one, 300-pound O'Neal was bigger than life—the biggest thing to hit Orlando since Disney World.

He was the National Basketball Association's own version of "Space Mountain." With O'Neal starring for the Orlando Magic, every day was going to be bigger and bouncier than the next.

The spirit of fun and exuberance usually associated with Disney World was now embodied in Orlando's new prominent citizen. O'Neal had come down to do some "chillin' with Mickey." Before long, he was the adopted son of the community, in some ways more popular than the Disney character. Mickey Mouse related mostly to the young. O'Neal related to all ages—especially the fans who follow the NBA.

He had slipped into the position of role model comfortably, although he wasn't totally in agreement with the concept. Athletes should be role models "to a certain extent," he said. "Like, when I was a kid, I could look up to Doctor J [Julius Erving], but if I needed some advice about the birds and the bees, I couldn't ask Doctor J. I had to call Mommy and Daddy. I mean, we should carry ourselves well on TV. We should not do things like beat our girlfriends up, do drugs or alcohol. Now, if all those kids lived with me, then I could be their role model."[2]

O'Neal wanted to feel a part of the community. Certainly, the community felt a part of him. He bought a home in an exclusive section of Orlando and installed video games and a stereo system that blasted his beloved rap music. One neighbor commented, "I could hear Shaquille's house before I saw it."[3]

O'Neal's generosity was the talk of the town and the nation. On Thanksgiving, he sponsored a "Shaqsgiving" to feed the homeless. During Christmas, he bought presents and played Santa Claus for underprivileged children. The new kid millionaire on the block also spread joy among his friends. To celebrate his new status, he took them to a water park. When the manager closed earlier than expected, O'Neal offered him $10,000 to keep the park open an extra hour.

Before Shaquille, the Magic had been overshadowed by Disney World. Shaquille's sparkling personality and entertaining play suddenly gave the Magic an identity. "Shaquille gives the Magic as a team more exposure," said Jack Swope, the Magic's executive vice president and assistant general manager. "He has taken us to another level nationally and expanded our local market tremendously."[4]

Because of O'Neal, the Magic suddenly became one of the highest-profile teams in the league. They made numerous appearances on television and brought in big crowds on the road. Orlando was box office magic. The season before, the Magic had ranked twenty-first in the twenty-seven-team NBA in road attendance. With O'Neal, they were second only behind the world-champion Chicago Bulls.

O'Neal was a celebrity before he was a pro. He signed an endorsement contract with the Reebok sneaker company before he played his first professional game. During his rookie season, a national marketing campaign propelled O'Neal into the public consciousness. O'Neal became the central figure in an advertising campaign by Reebok as the company sought to overtake Nike for the number-one spot in the sneaker industry.

O'Neal soon had his own business firm, a personalized logo (the name "SHAQ" superimposed over a silhouette of O'Neal dunking), a signature ball, his own line of clothing, and he also promoted soft drinks and toys, among other things. Shaq, easy to say in any language, was becoming an endorsement giant around the world.

Few other players had the camera-friendly personality of O'Neal. He appeared to be just what he was—a big kid having fun playing basketball. In the past, advertisers shied away from centers as endorsers. They didn't believe they were effective because their size made them intimidating and the average fan couldn't relate to them. Wilt Chamberlain once remarked that "nobody loves Goliath." But just about everyone loved the Shaq, thanks to a blend of power and innocence that made him appealing to young and old alike. O'Neal was described as a cross between the Terminator and Bambi.

Along with O'Neal, the NBA has enjoyed the fruits of his commercialism. His entrance into the league couldn't have come at a better time. The NBA had just lost Magic Johnson and Larry Bird, two of its biggest names. Michael Jordan's retirement shortly before the 1993–94 season left the league without another marquee attraction. The NBA was looking for new blood to lead the league into the new century and especially appeal to the new base of loyal fans. Many of the younger generation, exhilarated by Jordan's aeronautic creativity, had adopted the fast-paced sport.

The NBA had come from the dark ages to sports' front pages and it meant to stay there.

From its start in 1949, the league had ebbed and flowed in public acceptance.

George Mikan, the first of the super big men, was regarded as the savior of the league in its early years. The NBA, once overshadowed by college basketball, eventually took the spotlight with exceptional big men such as Wilt Chamberlain and Bill Russell in the 1960s. Kareem Abdul-Jabbar was the best-known big man in the 1970s and 1980s. Toward the end of his career, he was sharing the spotlight with Johnson, his teammate on the Los Angeles Lakers, and Bird, the star of the Boston Celtics.

At this time, the focus in the NBA's galaxy of stars had shifted to smaller players. Starting in the seventies, Julius Erving literally had brought a new level to the game with his sky-walking flair. Johnson and Bird helped to raise the popularity of the NBA in the eighties. And Jordan took the league to a higher plane in the nineties.

The NBA exploded under the guidance of David Stern, the media-friendly league commissioner. Runaway salaries, drug abuse, and waning fan support threatened the league in the early eighties. There was talk that the NBA would fold. Stern helped to turn things around. Stern joined the NBA as general counsel in 1978 and became commissioner in 1984. He was involved in virtually every important decision and policy in that period. He played a major role in the introduction of the salary cap that gave teams financial stability. He had a hand in drug testing, which helped clean up the image of the league. In 1983, the NBA became the first professional sports league to adopt a drug rehabilitation program. The merchandising and licensing of NBA products were also a priority during Stern's administration, as was the intelligent use of television.

Just as Pete Rozelle had marketed the National Football League in the 1960s, Stern recognized the importance of TV to promote the NBA in the 1980s. The league emphasized the big stars and the big games. Selling the individual talents of the players became just as important as selling the teams. Johnson, Bird, and later, Jordan became household names. Fortunately, they played in major media markets—Johnson in Los Angeles, Bird in Boston, and Jordan in Chicago.

Orlando wasn't in a major market. But it didn't matter. O'Neal was the center of a major marketing campaign by both the league and private business.

In O'Neal, the personality-driven NBA has the perfect player with which to link itself. O'Neal's game is based on strength. But he also has the agility and speed of smaller players, which makes him unusual for his size. More important, he plays the game joyfully and entertainingly. The fans have taken to O'Neal's boyish enthusiasm as they have to few other young players before him. He is a new breed of center, ideal for the modern age. A player to help lead the NBA to a new level and into a new century.

"I'm just out there working hard, having a lot of fun," O'Neal said. "I've been blessed. I just hope the fans enjoy watching me. I can't be great every night, but I can try."[5]

CAREER STATISTICS

COLLEGE/LOUISIANA STATE UNIVERSITY

YEAR	G	FG/FGA	PCT	FT/FTA	PCT	PTS	AVG	REB	AVG	AST	BLK	STL
1989–90	32	180/314	.573	85/153	.556	445	13.9	385	12.0	61	115	38
1990–91	28	312/497	.628	150/235	.638	774	27.6	411	14.7	45	140	41
1991–92	30	294/478	.615	134/254	.528	722	24.1	421	14.0	46	157	29
Totals	90	786/1289	.610	369/642	.575	1941	21.6	1217	13.5	152	412	108

PROFESSIONAL/ORLANDO MAGIC

YEAR	G	FG/FGA	PCT	FT/FTA	PCT	PTS	AVG	REB	AVG	AST	BLK	STL
1992–93	81	733/1304	.562	427/721	.592	1893	23.4	1122	13.9	152	286	60

SOURCE NOTES

1. SHAQ ATTACK

1. *Orlando Sentinel,* Feb. 8, 1993

2. ARMY BRAT

1. *Sports Illustrated,* May 18, 1992
2. *New York Times Magazine,* Nov. 15, 1992
3. *Florida Today,* Feb. 21, 1993
4. *The Oregonian,* Feb. 5, 1993
5. *Florida Today,* Feb. 21, 1993
6. *San Antonio Express-News,* Nov. 13, 1988
7. *New York Times Magazine,* Nov. 15, 1992
8. *New York Times Magazine,* Nov. 15, 1992
9. *Newsday,* August 1991
10. Author's interview
11. Author's interview
12. Author's interview

3. FLOWERING IN FULDA

1. Author's interview
2. Author's interview
3. Author's interview
4. *The Orange County Register,* Feb. 9, 1991
5. *Baton Rouge Advocate,* June 1992
6. Author's interview
7. Author's interview
8. Author's interview

4. A SOLDIER'S SON

1. Author's interview
2. Author's interview
3. Author's interview
4. Author's interview
5. Author's interview

5. TALL STORY

1. Author's interview
2. Author's interview
3. Author's interview
4. Author's interview
5. Author's interview
6. Author's interview
7. Author's interview
8. Author's interview
9. Author's interview
10. Author's interview
11. Author's interview
12. Author's interview
13. Author's interview
14. Author's interview

6. THE COLE EXPRESS

1. Author's interview
2. Author's interview
3. Author's interview
4. *Orange County Register,* Feb. 9, 1991
5. *San Antonio Express-News,* Sept. 15, 1988
6. *San Antonio Express-News,* Sept. 15, 1988
7. Author's interview

8. Author's interview
9. Author's interview
10. Author's interview
11. Author's interview
12. *San Antonio Express-News,* Jan. 5, 1989

7. THE SAMSON COMPLEX

1. Author's interview
2. *San Antonio Express-News,* March 12, 1989
3. *Austin American-Statesman,* March 10, 1989
4. Author's interview
5. *San Antonio Express-News,* March 12, 1989
6. *San Antonio Express-News,* March 19, 1989
7. Author's interview

8. COLLEGE BOUND

1. Author's interview
2. Author's interview
3. Author's interview
4. Author's interview
5. *San Antonio Light,* Nov. 10, 1988
6. Author's interview
7. *Sports Illustrated,* May 18, 1992
8. *San Antonio Express-News,* Nov. 10, 1988
9. Author's interview
10. *San Antonio Express-News,* March 1989

9. PERIOD OF ADJUSTMENT

1. Author's interview
2. Author's interview
3. Author's interview

4. *Shreveport Times,* April 3, 1992
5. Associated Press, Feb. 3, 1990

10. STANDING ALONE

1. *Chicago Tribune,* Feb. 17, 1991
2. *1991–92 NCAA Basketball Preview,* Fall 1991
3. Author's interview
4. Associated Press, Feb. 6, 1991
5. Author's interview
6. Author's interview
7. *Washington Post,* Jan. 20, 1991
8. *Inside Sports,* Nov. 1991
9. Author's interview
10. Author's interview
11. *Baton Rouge Advocate,* Feb. 20, 1992
12. Author's interview
13. Author's interview
14. Author's interview
15. Author's interview

11. EYE OF THE TIGER

1. *The Sporting News,* March 23, 1992
2. Associated Press, March 14, 1992
3. Associated Press, April 16, 1992
4. Associated Press, March 29, 1992
5. *Sports Illustrated,* Feb. 11, 1991
6. *The Sporting News,* March 23, 1992
7. Associated Press, March 14, 1992
8. Associated Press, March 14, 1992

12. GOING IN STYLE

1. Author's interview
2. Associated Press, March 20, 1992

3. Associated Press, April 3, 1992
4. *New Orleans Times-Picayune*, March 2, 1992
5. *Shreveport Times*, April 3, 1992
6. Author's interview
7. Author's interview
8. *Jet*, Dec. 9, 1991

13. MAKING A DECISION

1. Author's interview
2. Associated Press, April 4, 1992
3. Author's interview
4. Associated Press, April 4, 1992
5. *New Orleans Times-Picayune*, April 4, 1992

14. HITTING THE SHAQPOT

1. *Hoop Magazine*, December 1992
2. Author's interview
3. Author's interview
4. Author's interview
5. Author's interview

15. SUDDEN IMPACT

1. *New York Times*, Nov. 12, 1992
2. *Baltimore Sun*, Feb. 26, 1993
3. *New York Times*, Nov. 11, 1992
4. Author's interview
5. *Washington Post*, Nov. 22, 1992

16. ALL-STAR CONTROVERSY

1. *Orlando Sentinel*, Jan. 9, 1993
2. *Chicago Tribune*, Feb. 21, 1993

3. *Orlando Sentinel,* Feb. 4, 1993
4. *Orlando Sentinel,* Feb. 21, 1993
5. *Orlando Sentinel,* Feb. 21, 1993
6. *Orlando Sentinel,* Feb. 22, 1993
7. *Orlando Sentinel,* Feb. 22, 1993
8. *Orlando Sentinel,* Feb. 22, 1993

17. IN THE HUNT

1. Associated Press, April 8, 1993
2. Associated Press, April 18, 1993
3. Associated Press, April 18, 1993
4. Associated Press, April 21, 1993
5. Associated Press, April 22, 1993
6. Author's interview

18. ROOKIE OF THE YEAR

1. Associated Press, May 6, 1993
2. Author's interview
3. *Chicago Tribune,* Feb. 21, 1993
4. Author's interview
5. *Inside Sports,* June 1993
6. *Inside Sports,* June 1993

19. THE MAGIC KINGDOM

1. *Hoop Magazine,* Dec. 1992
2. *New York Times,* Nov. 15, 1992
3. Author's interview
4. *Magic Magazine,* Feb. 1993
5. *Tuff Stuff,* April 1993

INDEX

Abdul-Jabbar, Kareem, 51,
    58, 59, 84, 87–88, 92,
    112
  as Lew Alcindor, 58
America West Arena, 3
Anderson, Nick, 4, 82, 99,
    100, 101
Armato, Leonard, 84–85
Army brat, 5–11
  in Germany, 12–17, 18–23
Associated Press, 56

Backboards, breaking, 2–3,
    88–89, 100
Baker, Eric, 35, 36
Baker, Henry, 10–11
Barker, Tommy, 26
Barkley, Charles, 95
Basketball Congress Inter-
    national (BCI), 34
Bennett, Charles, 51, 64
Bird, Larry, 87, 111, 112, 113
Blocked shots
  college basketball, 53–54,
    57, 59, 60, 72, 73
  high school basketball, 20,
    36
  pro basketball, 95, 104–5
Bodybuilding, 34–35

Boston Celtics, 99–100
Bowie, Anthony, 2
Break-dancing, 15, 30
Brigham Young University
    (BYU) Cougars, 71–74
Bristow, Allan, 99
Brown, Dale, 67–68, 69–70,
    106
  advising O'Neal to turn
    pro, 69–70, 77, 78
  coaching O'Neal, 51–53,
    55, 56, 60, 62, 64, 72,
    73–74, 75
  recruiting O'Neal, 45–47,
    48–49
Business firm, 110

Campbell, Tony, 92
Catledge, Terry, 91
Cavallero, Joe, 30, 36
Celebrity status, 34, 61,
    110–11
Centers, 59, 94, 111
  NBA, 87–88
  new breed of, 113
  O'Neal as, 13, 34
Chamberlain, Wilt, 59, 86,
    87, 111, 112
  O'Neal compared to, 88
  salary, 90